CW00833558

Edexcel Certificate in
Mathematics
Edexcel International GCSE Mathematics A

Higher

Series Editors: Authors:

Andrew Manning   June Haighton

Paul Metcalf   Andrew Manning

   Ginette McManus

   Margaret Thornton

Revision Guide

Nelson Thornes

Text © June Haighton, Andrew Manning, Ginette McManus, Paul Metcalf,
Margaret Thornton 2013
Original illustrations © Nelson Thornes Ltd 2013

The rights of June Haighton, Andrew Manning, Ginette McManus, Paul Metcalf,
Margaret Thornton to be identified as author of this work has been asserted
by them in accordance with the Copyright, Designs and Patents Act 1988.

All rights reserved. No part of this publication may be reproduced or transmitted
in any form or by any means, electronic or mechanical, including photocopy,
recording or any information storage and retrieval system, without permission
in writing from the publisher or under licence from the Copyright Licensing
Agency Limited, of Saffron House, 6–10 Kirby Street, London, EC1N 8TS.

Any person who commits any unauthorised act in relation to this publication
may be liable to criminal prosecution and civil claims for damages.

Published in 2013 by:
Nelson Thornes Ltd
Delta Place
27 Bath Road
CHELTENHAM
GL53 7TH
United Kingdom

13 14 15 16 17 / 10 9 8 7 6 5 4 3 2 1

A catalogue record for this book is available from the British Library

ISBN 978 1 4085 2210 3

Cover photograph: Franck Boston/iStockphoto
Page make-up and illustrations by Tech-Set Ltd, Gateshead
Printed and bound in Spain by GraphyCems

NOTICE REGARDING ENDORSEMENT

In order to ensure that this resource offers high-quality support for the
associated Edexcel qualification, it has been through a review process by
the awarding body to confirm that it fully covers the teaching and learning
content of the specification or part of a specification at which it is aimed,
and demonstrates an appropriate balance between the development of subject
skills, knowledge and understanding, in addition to preparation for assessment.

While Nelson Thornes have made every attempt to ensure that advice on
the qualification and its assessment is accurate, the official specification and
associated assessment guidance materials are the only authoritative
source of information and should always be referred to for definitive guidance.

Edexcel examiners have not contributed to any sections in this resource
relevant to examination papers for which they have responsibility.

No material from this book will be used verbatim in any assessment set by
Edexcel.

Endorsement of this book does not mean that this book is required to achieve
this Edexcel qualification, nor does it mean that it is the only suitable material
available to support the qualification, and any resource lists produced by the
awarding body shall include this and other
appropriate resources.

Contents

Introduction

This revision guide has been written to support the Edexcel International GCSE and Certificate in Mathematics: Higher Tier and to help you revise for your exam. The authors have worked to ensure that the content reflects the syllabus and highlights the essential features of each topic area. Please note that topics have been grouped according to similarity, and some examples require knowledge of material that is covered later in the book.

Each chapter has the following features to make learning as interesting and effective as possible:

Learning outcomes

After this chapter you should be able to:

- factorise expressions

The **learning outcomes** at the start of the chapter give you an idea of the content of the chapter.

Revise: Each chapter is divided into a series of Revise sections to carefully take you through the required content. The Revise sections include key information which you should know for your exam.

Worked example: Each Revise includes a worked example or examples to illustrate and extend the content. You should work through the worked examples yourself and compare your answers with the solutions given.

Practise: Each Revise section is followed by a Practise section which includes questions that allow you to practise what you have just revised. The questions are carefully chosen to mirror the style of the exam papers.

Exam tip

Exam tip: Regular exam tips are included to help you avoid common errors and mistakes.

Practice exam questions

Practice exam questions appear at the end of the book. These offer further practice for your exams. You should work through the exam questions when you have completed the book.

Key words: The first time they appear in this book key words are highlighted in **bold blue** text. A definition can be found in the glossary section at the back of the book so that you can check the meaning of words and practise your mathematics vocabulary.

1 Angles

Learning outcomes

After this chapter you should be able to:

- use and interpret the geometrical terms: point, line, parallel, right angle, acute, obtuse and reflex angles, perpendicular, similarity, congruence
- use and interpret vocabulary of triangles, quadrilaterals, circles and polygons
- calculate unknown angles using:
  - angles at a point, on a straight line, between intersecting straight lines and parallel lines
  - angle properties of triangles, quadrilaterals, regular and irregular polygons
  - angles in a semicircle and between a tangent and radius of a circle
- use the relationships between areas and volumes of similar shapes
- identify and use properties of circles including angles at the centre and circumference, angles in the same segment, opposite angles of a cyclic quadrilateral and properties of tangents
- identify and use properties of chords including equal chords, intersecting chords and perpendicular bisectors of chords
- identify and use the alternate segment theorem.

Revise 1.1 Geometry

Angles

A full turn is 360° (**degrees**).

The **angle** between **perpendicular lines** is a **right angle**. This is 90° (a quarter turn).

An **acute** angle is less than 90°. An **obtuse** angle is greater than 90°, but less than 180°.

A **reflex** angle is greater than 180°, but less than 360°.

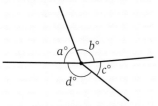

Angles at a point add up to 360°.

$a + b + c + d = 360$

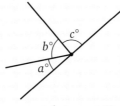

Angles on a straight line add up to 180°.

$a + b + c = 180$

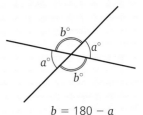

Vertically opposite angles are equal.

$b = 180 - a$

Parallel lines

Alternate angles are equal.	**Corresponding angles are equal.**	**Interior angles** add up to 180°.
$a = c$ and $b = d$	$a = e,\, b = f,\, c = g,$ and $d = h$	$a + d = 180$ and $b + c = 180$

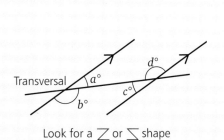

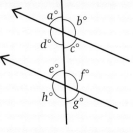

Look for a ⟋ or ⟍ shape   Look for a ⊢ or ⊣ shape   Look for a ⌐ or ⌐ shape

You must give the correct names in the examination, for example alternate angles, not Z angles.

Triangles and quadrilaterals

The angle sum of a triangle = 180°. The angle sum of a quadrilateral = 360°.

Special triangles and quadrilaterals

The properties that you should know are shown below.

Equilateral triangle   **Isosceles triangle**   **Scalene triangle**   **Right-angled triangle**

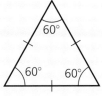

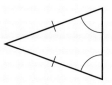

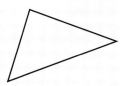

All sides equal Each angle is 60°	Two equal sides Two equal angles	All sides different All angles different	One right angle and two acute angles

Square   **Rectangle**   **Rhombus**

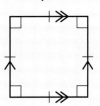

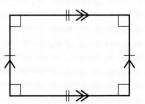

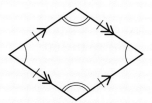

All sides equal Opposite sides parallel Each angle is 90°	Opposite sides equal Opposite sides parallel Each angle is 90°	All sides equal Opposite sides parallel Opposite angles equal

Parallelogram	Trapezium	Kite
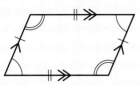	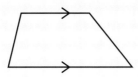	
Opposite sides equal Opposite sides parallel Opposite angles equal	One pair of parallel sides (In an isosceles trapezium the non-parallel sides are equal)	Two pairs of adjacent sides equal One pair of equal angles

You also need to know about the symmetries of these shapes (see Revise 9.1).

Congruence and similarity

Congruent shapes are exactly the same shape and size. They have corresponding angles that are equal and corresponding sides of the same length.

Similar shapes are the same shape. They have equal angles and corresponding sides are in the same ratio.

If corresponding lengths in the two similar shapes are in the ratio $a : b$

- the areas are in the ratio $a^2 : b^2$
- the volumes are in the ratio $a^3 : b^3$.

Worked examples

Triangles and quadrilaterals

Find the values of a and b. Give reasons for your answers.

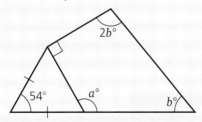

Solution

The triangle is isosceles with equal angles $= \dfrac{180° - 54°}{2} = 63°$ ← Angle sum of a triangle = 180°.

$a = 180 - 63 = 117$ ← Angles on a straight line add up to 180°.

$b + 2b + 90 + 117 = 360$ ← Angle sum of a quadrilateral = 360°.

$3b = 360 - 207$

$b = 153 \div 3$

$b = 51$

Parallel lines and similar triangles

a In the diagram $AD = 21$ cm, $DE = 36$ cm and $BC = 24$ cm.
Calculate the length of BD.

b The area of triangle ADE is 216 cm².
Calculate the area of trapezium $BCED$.

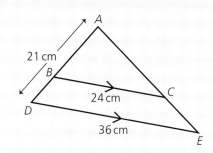

Solution

a Angle ADE = angle ABC ← Corresponding angles are equal since BC is parallel to DE.

Angle DAE = angle BAC ← Since these are the same angle.

Angle AED = angle ACB ← Corresponding angles are equal since BC is parallel to DE.

So triangles $\dfrac{ABC}{ADE}$ are similar and corresponding sides are in the same ratio.

$\dfrac{AB}{AD} = \dfrac{BC}{DE}$ gives $\dfrac{AB}{21} = \dfrac{24}{36}$ ← Putting the unknown side as the numerator makes the working easier.

Cancelling gives $\dfrac{AB}{21} = \dfrac{2}{3}$

so $AB = \dfrac{2 \times 21}{3} = 14$ cm

$BD = AD - AB = 21 - 14 = 7$ cm

b Lengths in triangles ABC and ADE are in the ratio $2 : 3$, so areas are in the ratio $2^2 : 3^2 = 4 : 9$

$\dfrac{\text{Area of triangle } ABC}{\text{Area of triangle } ADE} = \dfrac{4}{9}$ so $\dfrac{\text{Area of triangle } ABC}{216} = \dfrac{4}{9}$

Area of triangle $ABC = \dfrac{4}{9} \times 216 = 96$ cm²

Area of trapezium $BCED$ = Area of triangle ADE − Area of triangle ABC

$= 216 - 96 = 120$ cm²

Revise 1.2 Angle properties

Angle sums of polygons

Any **polygon** can be split into triangles.

The number of triangles is two less than the number of sides.

For example, a pentagon has 5 sides. It can be split into 3 triangles.

Angle sum of any polygon = (number of sides − 2) × 180°
= (2n − 4) right angles.

A **regular** polygon has all sides equal and all angles equal.

So the angle sum of a pentagon = 3 × 180°

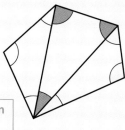

The table gives the angles of some regular polygons.

Name of polygon	Number of sides	Number of triangles	Sum of interior angles	When the polygon is regular, each angle =
Triangle	3	1	$1 \times 180° = 180°$	$180° \div 3 = 60°$
Quadrilateral	4	2	$2 \times 180° = 360°$	$360° \div 4 = 90°$
Pentagon	5	3	$3 \times 180° = 540°$	$540° \div 5 = 108°$
Hexagon	6	4	$4 \times 180° = 720°$	$720° \div 6 = 120°$
Heptagon	7	5	$5 \times 180° = 900°$	$900° \div 7 = 128\frac{4}{7}°$
Octagon	8	6	$6 \times 180° = 1080°$	$1080° \div 8 = 135°$
Nonagon	9	7	$7 \times 180° = 1260°$	$1260° \div 9 = 140°$
Decagon	10	8	$8 \times 180° = 1440°$	$1440° \div 10 = 144°$

> A regular triangle is equilateral.

> A regular quadrilateral is a square.

The sum of the exterior angles of any polygon = 360°.

At each vertex of the polygon,
interior angle + exterior angle = 180°.

For example, each exterior angle of a
regular hexagon = $360° \div 6 = 60°$
and each interior angle = $180° - 60° = 120°$.

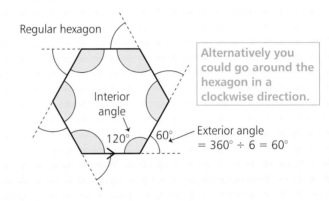

Regular hexagon

Interior angle

$120°$ $60°$

> Alternatively you could go around the hexagon in a clockwise direction.

Exterior angle
= $360° \div 6 = 60°$

Exam tip

Using the sum of the exterior angles equals 360° is often the quickest way to solve problems involving polygons.

Worked example

Polygons

The diagram shows part of a regular polygon.

Each interior angle of the polygon is 144°.

How many sides has this polygon?

$144°$ $144°$

Solution

The exterior angle of this polygon $= 180° - 144° = 36°$.

> Angles on a straight line add up to 180°.

The number of exterior angles $= 360° \div 36° = 10$.

> Since the sum of the exterior angles of a polygon is 360°.

The polygon has 10 sides.

Revise 1.3 Circle properties

Circle properties

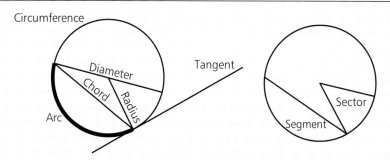

The angle subtended by an **arc** (or **chord**) at the centre of a circle is twice the angle subtended at any point on the circumference.

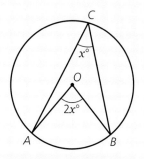

This means that the angle subtended at the circumference by a diameter is a right angle. In other words, the angle in a **semicircle** is always 90°.

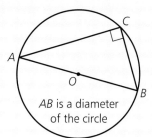

AB is a diameter of the circle

Angles in the same segment are equal.

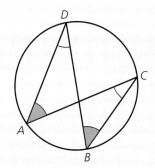

A **cyclic quadrilateral** is one where all four vertices lie on the circumference of a circle.

The opposite angles of a cyclic quadrilateral add up to 180°.

$p + r = 180$
$q + s = 180$

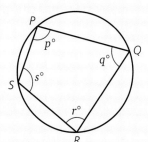

A **tangent** is always perpendicular to
the radius drawn at the point where the
tangent touches the circle.

Tangents from an external point are equal
in length.

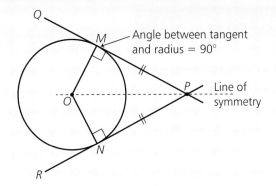

Angle between tangent
and radius = 90°

Line of
symmetry

The perpendicular from the centre to a chord bisects the chord.
The perpendicular bisector of a chord passes through the
centre of the circle.

The perpendicular *OM* cuts
the chord *AB* in half.
AM = MB.

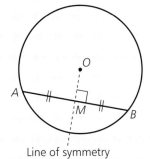

Line of symmetry

Equal chords are equidistant from
the centre of the circle.

AB = CD
so *OM = ON*

Line of
symmetry

The angle between a tangent and chord is equal to the angle in the alternate segment.

Angle *CBE* = angle *BAC*.
Also, angle *ABD* = angle
ACB

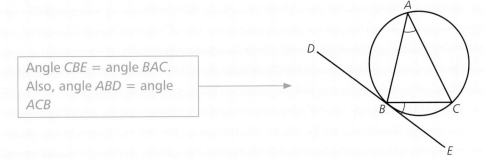

If two chords *AB* and *CD* intersect at *N*, then *AN* × *NB* = *CN* × *ND*

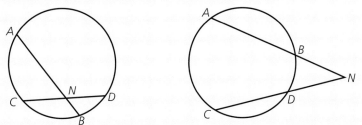

Worked examples

Circle chord properties

A circle, centre O and diameter 12 cm, has a chord AB of length 7.2 cm.

Find the distance from O to AB.

Solution

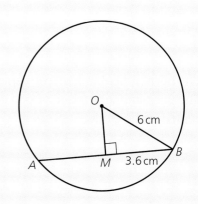

The diagram shows the circle and the chord AB.

OB = the radius of the circle = 12 cm ÷ 2 = 6 cm.

M is the midpoint of the chord with MB = 7.2 cm ÷ 2 = 3.6 cm.

Using Pythagoras (see Revise 13.1) in triangle OMB

$OM^2 = 6^2 - 3.6^2 = 36 - 12.96 = 23.04$

$OM = \sqrt{23.04} = 4.8$ cm

Circle angle properties

P, Q, R and S lie on a circle, centre O.
TPU and TSV are tangents to the circle.

Find the size of the angles marked by letters.

Give reasons for your answers.

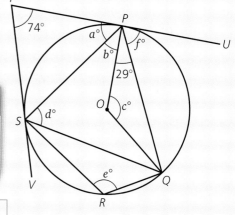

> #### Exam tip
>
> Remember that equal tangents and equal radii of a circle often give useful isosceles triangles.
>
> Note 'radii' is the plural of 'radius'.

Solution

$a = \dfrac{180 - 74}{2} = 53$ ◄—— TP and TS are equal tangents, so a° is one of the equal angles of isosceles triangle TPS.

$b = 90 - 53 = 37$ ◄—— The angle between tangent TP and radius OP is 90°.

$c = 180 - 2 \times 29 = 122$ ◄—— OP and OQ are radii, so triangle OPQ is isosceles with two angles of 29°.

$d = 122 \div 2 = 61$ ◄—— Angle POQ at the centre is twice angle PSQ, the angle at the circumference on the same arc PQ.

$e = 180 - (b + 29)$ ◄—— Opposite angles of cyclic quadrilateral PQRS add up to 180°.
$\quad = 180 - 66 = 114$

$f = d = 61$ ◄—— d is in the alternate segment

> Often there is more than one way to find an angle. Here f could be found by using the fact that the angle between tangent PU and radius OP is 90°.

Practise 1.1 – 1.3

1 **a** *ABCD* is a parallelogram. Angle *ABC* = 112°.

Find the sizes of the other angles of the parallelogram, giving reasons for your answers.

b *PQRS* is a quadrilateral. *PQ* = *PS* and *QR* = *SR*.

The diagonals *PR* and *QS* intersect at a point *T*.

i Draw a sketch of *PQRS* and write down its name.

ii Name an angle that is equal to angle *PQR*.

iii Name a triangle that is congruent to triangle *RST*.

2 **a** **i** Work out the size of the interior angles of a regular polygon that has 20 sides.

ii Use a different method to check your answer to part **a i**.

b A regular polygon has interior angles of 156°. Find the number of sides of the polygon.

c A pentagon has two right angles. The other angles are equal to each other.

Work out the size of these angles.

3 **a** Find the sizes of the following angles. Give reasons for your answers.

i Angle *STR*   **iii** Angle *PRQ*

ii Angle *PQR*   **iv** Angle *RPQ*

b *PQ* = 25 cm, *QR* = 15 cm and *SR* = 6 cm.
Calculate the length of *TS*.

c The area of triangle *PQR* is 150 cm².
Find the area of triangle *TSR*.

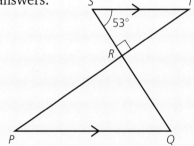

4 The radius of a circle is 6.5 cm long.

The distance from the centre of this circle to a chord is 2.5 cm.

Calculate the length of the chord.

5 *A*, *B* and *C* lie on a circle, centre *O*, with diameter 20 cm.

AB = *BC* and the length of the tangent *CD* is 15 cm.

Calculate the length of: **a** *OD*   **b** *AB*.

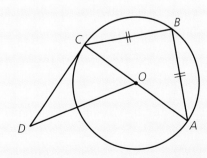

6 Find the size of each angle marked by a letter. Give a reason for each answer.

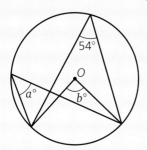 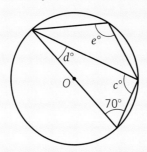 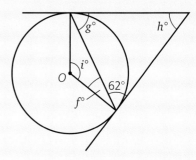

7 Find the size of each angle marked by a letter. Give a reason for each answer.

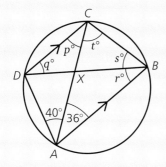 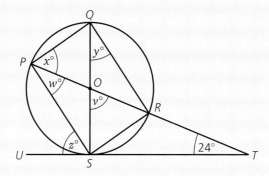

8 *A, B, C* and *D* lie on a circle. *AC* and *BD* intersect at *X*.

Angle *ABX* = 27° and angle *AXB* = 99°.

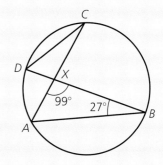

a Write down the size of angle *ACD*.

Give a reason for your answer.

b Find the size of angle *BDC*. Give reasons for your answer.

c *AX* = 10.3 cm, *BX* = 18.6 cm and *CX* = 12.4 cm.

Calculate the length of *DX*.

d The area of triangle *ABX* is 94.6 cm².

Calculate the area of triangle *CDX*.

9 a Each interior angle of a regular polygon is 5 times each exterior angle.
Calculate the number of sides of the polygon.

b *ABCDEFGH* is an octagon.
The interior angle *B* is 6° greater than the interior angle *A*.
The interior angle *C* is 6° greater than the interior angle *B*, and so on, with each of the next interior angles 6° greater than the previous one.
Calculate the size of interior angle *A*.

10 *A*, *B*, *C* and *D* lie on a circle, centre *O*.
SAT is the tangent at *A* and is parallel to *OB*.
Angle *TAB* = 47° and angle *COB* = 116°.

Calculate the size of angle *ADC*.

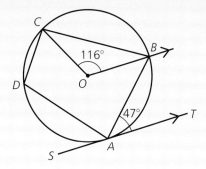

11 Two similar bottles have heights that are in the ratio 3 : 4.

  a The surface area of the larger bottle is 512 cm².

  Calculate the surface area of the smaller bottle.

  b The volume of the smaller bottle is 324 cm³.

  Calculate the volume of the larger bottle.

12 The surface area of a ball is 36π cm². The volume of this ball is 36π cm³.
The diameter of a larger ball is 50% greater than that of the first ball.
Calculate the surface area and volume of this larger ball.
Leave your answers in terms of π.

13 *A*, *B* and *C* lie on a circle, centre *O*.
DE is the tangent to the circle at the point *C*.
Angle *BAC* = 58° and angle *ACE* = 54°.
Calculate the size of angle *ABO*.

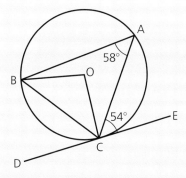

Learning outcomes

After this chapter you should be able to:

- identify and use:
  - natural numbers, integers, rational and irrational numbers, real numbers
  - common factors and common multiples, prime numbers, square numbers
- put numbers in order of size and use the symbols $=$, $\neq$, $<$, $>$, $\leqslant$, $\geqslant$
- convert between fractions, decimals (including recurring decimals) and percentages
- add, subtract, multiply and divide decimals and fractions, including those with mixed numbers
- solve problems involving fractions and decimals
- apply operations in the correct order when calculating
- simplify ratios, divide a quantity in a given ratio and know the difference between ratio and proportion
- solve questions involving direct and inverse proportion and use algebraic techniques to find unknown quantities
- use the unitary method and the multiplier method
- solve questions involving the common measures of rate of change.

Revise 2.1 Basic number

The structure of numbers

Natural numbers are the counting numbers 1, 2, 3, 4, 5, …

Integers are all the numbers …, -5, -4, -3, -2, -1, 0, 1, 2, 3, 4, 5, …

Rational numbers are all the numbers that can be written in the form $\dfrac{p}{q}$, where p and q are integers.

Integers, terminating decimals and recurring decimals are rational numbers.

Irrational numbers are all the numbers that *cannot* be written in the form $\dfrac{p}{q}$.

The **real numbers** are all the rational numbers and irrational numbers.

The **Venn diagram** shows the relationship between these numbers.

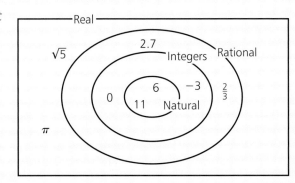

Ordering numbers

To order integers, draw or imagine a number line.

The numbers increase from left to right.

Each digit in an integer or decimal has a place value. For example, in the number 345.127, there are 345 whole ones as this is the number to the left of the decimal point. The place values are Hundreds, Tens and Units, so there are 3 Hundreds, 4 Tens and 5 Units. To the right of the decimal point are the parts of a whole one. The place values are tenths, hundredths and thousandths.

To order decimals, write them in a table with a separate column for each place value.

To order 3.45, 3.6 and 3.427

U	.	t	h	th
3	.	4	5	
3	.	6		
3	.	4	2	7

All three numbers have 3 units.

3.6 has the most tenths, so is the largest.

3.45 has more hundredths than 3.427, so 3.45 is larger than 3.427

From largest to smallest, the correct order is 3.6, 3.45, 3.427

Using the symbols =, ≠, <, >, ≤, ≥

- When two quantities are equal, you can show it with the equals sign, =.

- If quantities are not equal, you can use the 'is not equal to' sign, ≠.

- You could also write $\sqrt{15} < 4$, meaning '$\sqrt{15}$ is less than 4'.

- Also $\sqrt[3]{10} > 2$, $\sqrt[3]{10}$ is greater than 2.

- ≤ means 'is less than or equal to'.

- ≥ means 'is greater than or equal to'.

Types of number

Multiples, factors, primes and squares

A **multiple** is a number in the multiplication table of another number.

Multiples of 4 are 4, 8, 12, 16, 20, …

A **factor** is a number that divides exactly into another number with no remainder.

1, 2, 3, 4, 6 and 12 are factors of 12, because 12 can be divided exactly by 1, 2, 3, 4, 6, and 12.

A **prime number** is a number that has exactly two factors, 1 and itself.

2, 3 and 5 are prime numbers.

Square numbers are the result of multiplying an integer by itself.

Examples are 9 (= 3 × 3), 100 (= 10 × 10) and 25 (= 5 × 5).

Exam tip

- 1 is not a prime number as it has only one factor.

- 2 is the only even prime number.

Common multiples and common factors

A common multiple of two numbers is a number that is a multiple of both.

The **lowest common multiple (LCM)** of two numbers is the smallest number that is a multiple of both.

A common factor of two numbers is a number that is a factor of both.

The **highest common factor (HCF)** of two numbers is the largest number that is a factor of both.

Worked examples

Ordering numbers

Write these in order, starting with the smallest:

$$\sqrt{10} \qquad 3\frac{1}{7} \qquad \pi \qquad 3.15$$

Solution

Write these numbers as decimals:

$$\sqrt{10} = 3.1622\ldots \qquad 3\frac{1}{7} = 3.1428\ldots \qquad \pi = 3.1415\ldots \qquad 3.15 = 3.15$$

Order the decimals:

$$3.1415\ldots \qquad 3.1428\ldots \qquad 3.15 \qquad 3.1622\ldots$$

Then order the numbers in the original form:

$$\pi \qquad 3\frac{1}{7} \qquad 3.15 \qquad \sqrt{10}$$

Factors, multiples, primes and squares

Markus says that all numbers have an even number of factors.

Monika says that no prime numbers are square numbers.

Moshe says that the lowest common multiple of 56 and 42 is 336.

Only one person is correct. Who is correct?

Show that the other two are wrong.

Solution

Markus is wrong. All square numbers have an odd number of factors, e.g. the factors of 4 are 1, 2 and 4.

Monika is correct. A square number is made by multiplying a number by itself and so it cannot be prime.

Moshe is incorrect. 336 is a common multiple of 56 and 42, but 168 is the lowest common multiple.

Revise 2.2 Decimals, fractions and percentages

Working with decimals

To add or subtract decimals you must make sure that you line up the decimal points.

Put 0s in any spaces to avoid making mistakes.

You can multiply decimals using the grid method or the column method. Begin both methods by taking out the decimal point. When you have finished the calculation, use your rough estimate to put back in the decimal point.

Exam tip

When using a calculator, always do a rough estimate in your head. Make sure your answer is close to your rough estimate. If it isn't then you have made a mistake.

To divide decimals, rewrite the division so that you are always dividing by a whole number. Use equivalent fractions to do this.

For example, $24.72 \div 0.06 = \dfrac{24.72}{0.06}$

$$= \dfrac{2472}{6} \qquad \longleftarrow \boxed{\text{Multiply both numbers by 100.}}$$

$$= 2472 \div 6 = 412$$

Fractions

All fractions can be written in the form $\dfrac{a}{b}$.

$$\dfrac{2}{3}$$

The numerator is the number on the top of a fraction

The denominator is the number on the bottom

When fractions have different denominators, they are difficult to compare, so change them to **equivalent fractions**.

Equivalent fractions can be simplified by cancelling down or rewriting them in their **simplest form**.

This is done by dividing or multiplying both the numerator and the denominator by the same number. This is repeated until the fraction has the smallest possible whole number in its numerator and denominator.

Changing fractions to decimals

To change a fraction to a decimal, divide the numerator by the denominator.

Sometimes the division does not work out exactly, and you are left with a **recurring decimal**. Recurring decimals are shown by placing dots above a number or numbers that repeat.

For example, $0.\dot{6}$ is said as '6 recurring' and is a short way of writing 0.666666 …

Also, $0.21\dot{4}1\dot{6}$ is a short way of writing 0.21416416416 …

Changing decimals to fractions

To change a decimal to a fraction, you need to consider the place value of each digit.

Thousands	Hundreds	Tens	Units	.	Tenths	Hundredths	Thousandths
1000	100	10	1	.	0.1 or $\frac{1}{10}$	0.01 or $\frac{1}{100}$	0.001 or $\frac{1}{1000}$

In the number 3.42, the last digit is in the hundredths place, so the decimal part can be written as hundredths, $3.42 = 3\frac{42}{100} = 3\frac{21}{50}$

To change a recurring decimal to a fraction, multiply the decimal by an appropriate power of 10 so that subtracting removes the recurring part.

To change $0.\dot{2}1\dot{6}$ to a decimal:

Let $x = 0.216216216\ldots$

Then $1000x = 216.216216\ldots$ Multiplying by $10^3 = 1000$ as there are 3 repeating digits

$\qquad x = 0.216216\ldots$

$\quad 999x = 216$ $\longleftarrow$ By subtracting

$\qquad x = \frac{216}{999}$ $\longleftarrow$ Dividing both sides by 999

$\qquad x = \frac{24}{111} = \frac{8}{37}$ $\longleftarrow$ Cancelling by 9 and then by 3

Changing percentages to fractions and decimals

One per cent (1%) means '1 out of every 100'.

A percentage is a number of hundredths.

To change a percentage to a fraction (or decimal), divide by 100.

To change a fraction or a decimal to a percentage

To change a fraction (or decimal) to a percentage, multiply by 100.

You can use what you know about equivalent fractions to rewrite a fraction with a denominator of 100.

Working with fractions

Addition and subtraction

To add and subtract fractions their denominators must be the same.

If the denominators are different, then you need to change them to a common denominator.

The common denominator is a multiple of all the denominators. If possible, use the lowest common denominator.

Change the fractions to equivalent fractions by multiplying the numerator and denominator by the same number.

Your calculations may involve **mixed numbers**.

Mixed numbers are fractions that consist of two parts: a whole number part and a fractional part.

When you add or subtract mixed numbers, you deal with the whole numbers and the fractions separately.

Exam tip

Multiplying the denominators together will always give a common denominator, but it will not always be the lowest one.

Improper fractions are fractions where the numerator is larger than the denominator.

To change an improper fraction to a mixed number, divide the numerator by the denominator to find the number of whole ones. For example, $\frac{20}{7} = 20 \div 7 = 2$ with a remainder of 6, so $\frac{20}{7} = 2\frac{6}{7}$.

To change a mixed number to an improper fraction, multiply the number of whole ones by the denominator to convert the whole ones, and then add the numerator.

$$3\frac{4}{5} = \frac{3 \times 5 + 4}{5} = \frac{19}{5}$$

Multiplication and division

To multiply fractions, convert any mixed numbers to improper fractions.

Then cancel down if possible by dividing a numerator and a denominator by a common factor.

Next, multiply the numerators together and the denominators together.

If the answer is an improper fraction, change it to a mixed number.

To multiply a fraction by an integer, write the integer as a fraction over 1, e.g. $7 = \frac{7}{1}$.

To divide by a fraction you must *multiply* by the **reciprocal** of the fraction that follows the division sign.

To find the reciprocal of a fraction, turn it upside down. Change mixed numbers into improper fractions before turning them upside down.

To be awarded full marks in questions on fractions, working must be shown.

Ordering operations

Use **BIDMAS** for calculations involving more than one operation.

B Brackets

I Indices (powers: squares, cubes, …)

D Division
M Multiplication
} Do these together, working from left to right

A Addition
S Subtraction
} Do these together, working from left to right

Worked examples

Working with fractions

Calculate, showing full working:

a $2\frac{3}{4} + 1\frac{2}{3}$ **b** $4\frac{1}{3} - 1\frac{5}{6}$ **c** $2\frac{1}{2} \times 1\frac{2}{5}$ **d** $3\frac{1}{5} \div 1\frac{1}{3}$

Solution

a $2\frac{3}{4} + 1\frac{2}{3}$

$= 3\frac{3}{4} + \frac{2}{3}$ ← Add the whole ones.

$= 3\frac{9}{12} + \frac{8}{12}$ ← 12 is the lowest common denominator of 4 and 3.

$= 3\frac{17}{12}$

$= 4\frac{5}{12}$ ← $\frac{17}{12} = 17 \div 12 = 1\frac{5}{12}$

b $4\frac{1}{3} - 1\frac{5}{6}$

$= 3\frac{1}{3} - \frac{5}{6}$ ← Subtract the whole ones.

$= 3\frac{2}{6} - \frac{5}{6}$ ← 6 is the lowest common denominator of 3 and 6.

$= 2\frac{8}{6} - \frac{5}{6}$ ← As $2 - 5$ gives a negative answer, split a whole one into $\frac{6}{6}$

$= 2\frac{3}{6}$

$= 2\frac{1}{2}$ ← Simplify by cancelling by 3.

c $2\frac{1}{2} \times 1\frac{2}{5}$

$= \frac{5}{2} \times \frac{7}{5}$ ← Change to improper fractions.

$= \frac{\cancel{5}^1}{2} \times \frac{7}{\cancel{5}_1}$ ← Cancel the numerator and denominator of 5 by dividing by 5.

$= \frac{7}{2}$ ← Multiply numerators and multiply denominators.

$= 3\frac{1}{2}$ ← Change back to mixed number.

d $3\frac{1}{5} \div 1\frac{1}{3}$

$= \frac{16}{5} \div \frac{4}{3}$ ← Change to improper fractions.

$= \frac{16}{5} \times \frac{3}{4}$ ← Turn second fraction upside down and multiply.

$= \frac{\cancel{16}^4}{5} \times \frac{3}{\cancel{4}_1}$ ← Cancel the numerator (16) and denominator (4) by dividing by 4.

$= \frac{12}{5}$ ← Multiply numerators and multiply denominators.

$= 2\frac{2}{5}$ ← Change back to mixed number.

Recurring decimals

Change the recurring decimal $0.\dot{2}\dot{4}$ to a fraction in its lowest terms.

Solution

Let $x = 0.242424\ldots$

> The first two digits repeat, so multiply both sides of the equation by 100.

$$100x = 24.242424\ldots$$

> The decimal parts line up underneath each other.

$$x = 0.242424\ldots$$

$$99x = 24$$

> So on subtracting they will disappear.

So $\qquad x = \dfrac{24}{99} = \dfrac{8}{33}$

Therefore $0.\dot{2}\dot{4} = \dfrac{8}{33}$

Revise 2.3 Ratio and proportion

Simplifying ratios

Fractions and percentages can be used to describe proportions, but ratios can only be used to compare like quantities. A ratio is written using a colon, e.g. $2 : 3$.

The order of a ratio is important.

A **proportion** compares one quantity with the total amount and is written as a fraction, e.g. $\frac{4}{5}$.

Ratios can be simplified by multiplying or dividing each part of the ratio by the same amount. This means that they can be simplified in the same way as for fractions.

A ratio is in its **simplest form** when it contains the smallest possible whole numbers.

You may be asked to write ratios in the form $1 : n$ or $n : 1$. These are called **unitary ratios**. For these ratios, you may leave decimals or fractions in the answer.

Dividing quantities in a given ratio

Some money is to be shared between two sisters in the ratio $x : y$.

The money must be divided into $(x + y)$ parts.

One sister gets x parts and the other gets y parts.

Example 1: Share $30 in the ratio $5 : 7$.

Solution: Divide $30 into 12 parts, as $5 + 7 = 12$.

$$\$30 \div 12 = \$2.50$$

The amounts are $5 \times \$2.50 = \$12.50$ and $7 \times \$2.50 = \$17.50$

Check that both of these answers add up to the total amount: $\$12.50 + \$17.50 = \$30$.

Example 2: A map has a scale of $1 : 50\,000$.

Two towns are 9 km apart.

How far apart are they on the map?

Solution: $9\,\text{km} = 9000\,\text{m} = 900\,000\,\text{cm}$

This is 50 000 parts in the ratio.

So one part $= 900\,000\,\text{cm} \div 50\,000 = 90\,\text{cm} \div 5 = 18\,\text{cm}$

So on the map, they are 18 cm apart.

Exam tip

If you are asked to divide an amount in a given ratio, you can check your answer using this method:

- add together all the parts of your answer
- the sum should be the total value given in the original question.

Using ratios

The unitary method

To use the **unitary method**, calculate the value of one single unit, and then multiply to get the required answer.

For example, to find the cost of 9 glasses if 5 glasses cost $4:

> one glass costs $4 \div 5 = \$0.80$
>
> 9 glasses cost $9 \times \$0.80 = \$7.20$

Direct proportion is when one variable increases in proportion with another variable.

For example, if the number of items increases, then so does the cost.

When two quantities x and y are directly proportional, the graph showing this is a straight line through the origin.

Inverse proportion is when one variable increases as the other decreases.

For example, a photographer charges the same price for all photographs with the same area.

If a rectangle has a fixed area, then if the length increases the width decreases.

These rectangles all have an area of $6\,\text{cm}^2$.

The length is inversely proportional to the width because if the width is multiplied by 2, the length is divided by 2.

Each rectangle has its bottom left-hand corner at the origin.

The top right-hand corners have coordinates (x, y) such that $xy = 6$.

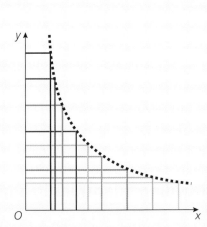

The dotted line shows the shape of a graph of two quantities that are inversely proportional.

The multiplier method

To use the multiplier method, you multiply the quantity by the fraction representing the ratio.

For example, the ratio $3 : 2$ can be used to form two fractions $\frac{3}{2}$ and $\frac{2}{3}$.

If you multiply by $\frac{3}{2}$, you will be increasing in the ratio $3 : 2$.

If you multiply by $\frac{2}{3}$, you will be decreasing in the ratio $2 : 3$.

Compound measures

A compound measure is made up of two other measures.

Speed, in kilometres per hour, is a compound measure made up from a measure of length (kilometres) and a measure of time (hours).

Problems that include compound measures can be answered using a formula triangle.

Average speed (km/h) $= \dfrac{\text{distance (km)}}{\text{time (hours)}}$, or $S = \dfrac{D}{T}$

This can be written in a triangle:

To calculate a time, cover up the T:

$$\text{time} = \frac{D}{S}$$

To calculate a distance, cover up the D:

$$\text{distance} = S \times T$$

Always check that the units given in the question match each other. If not, change these before you start your calculations.

Direct and inverse proportion

y is **directly proportional** to x or $y \propto x$, if $y = kx$ (where k is a constant)

k is known as the **constant of proportionality**.

y is **inversely proportional** to x, or $y \propto \dfrac{1}{x}$, if $y = \dfrac{k}{x}$ (where k is a constant)

y can also be directly or inversely proportional to the square, cube, square root, ... of x.

If y is inversely proportional to the square of x, then $y \propto \dfrac{1}{x^2}$ or $y = \dfrac{k}{x^2}$.

If $y = 2$ when $x = 3$, then $2 = \dfrac{k}{3^2}$, or $k = 18$.

So $y = \dfrac{18}{x^2}$.

Worked examples

Dividing quantities in a given ratio

A charity receives money from three different places: the government, local businesses and from collections at the local supermarket. This money is in the ratio $4:5:2$.

In one month, the total money received is $6160.

How much does the charity receive from the local supermarket collections?

Solution

Government : businesses : supermarket $= 4:5:2$

There are $4 + 5 + 2 = 11$ parts altogether.

$\frac{1}{11}$ of the money received $= \frac{1}{11} \times \$6160 = \$560$

So the money from the supermarket collections $= \frac{2}{11} \times \$6160 = 2 \times \$560 = \$1120$

You can check this answer. Work out all three different amounts and add them up. The total should be $6160.

Money from government $= \frac{4}{11} \times \$6160 = \$2240$

Money from businesses $= \frac{5}{11} \times \$6160 = \$2800$

Money from supermarket $= \frac{2}{11} \times \$6160 = \$1120$

Total $= \$2240 + \$2800 + \$1120 = \$6160$

Proportion

If p varies inversely as q, and $p = 10$ when $q = 6$, find:

a p, when $q = 16$ **b** q, when $p = 1.5$

Solution

a $\quad p \propto \dfrac{1}{q}$

then

$\quad p = \dfrac{k}{q}$ where k is a constant.

When $p = 10$, $q = 6$, so

$\quad 10 = \dfrac{k}{6}$

$\quad 60 = k$ ◄————————————————————— Multiply both sides by 6.

$\quad k = 60$

The equation becomes

$\quad p = \dfrac{60}{q}$

Substituting $q = 16$ into this equation gives:

$\quad p = \dfrac{60}{16}$

$\quad p = 3.75$

b Substituting $p = 1.5$ into the equation gives:

$$1.5 = \frac{60}{q}$$ ◄──────────────── Multiply both sides by q.

$$1.5q = 60$$ ◄──────────────── Divide both sides by 1.5

$$q = \frac{60}{1.5}$$

$$q = 40$$

Practise 2.1 – 2.3

1 Calculate: $\dfrac{2.4 + 1.2^2 \times 40}{5^2 - 10 \div 2}$

2 On a map, a length of 1 km is represented by a length of 8 mm.

Find the ratio of the length on the map to the actual length in the form $1 : n$.

3 Find the lowest common multiple of 28 and 35.

4 Write these numbers in order of size, largest first.

$$28\% \qquad \frac{2}{7} \qquad 0.27 \qquad \frac{3}{11}$$

5 $a \geqslant 6$ and $b < 2$.

Put a tick in a column to say whether these statements must be true, might be true or cannot be true.

	Must be true	Might be true	Cannot be true
$a > b$			
$a \div b = 3$			
$a + b > 4$			
$a - b > 4$			

6 Write $0.7\dot{2}$ as a fraction in its simplest form.

7 a is inversely proportional to the square of b.

Use this information to complete the table:

a	4	1		5.76
b	3		2	

8 Show that:

a $3\frac{3}{4} + 2\frac{3}{5} = 6\frac{7}{20}$
b $2\frac{5}{6} \div 1\frac{1}{3} = 2\frac{1}{8}$

Show all stages in your working.

9 A local farmer picks 5 boxes of oranges in 3 hours.

    a How long would it take him to pick 4 boxes?

On another day, he picked 36 boxes of oranges in 10 hours.
The next day, he must pick another 36 boxes.
This time he has two friends to help him.

    b Assuming that all three work at the same rate as the farmer did on his own, how long will it take them?

Give your answers to both parts, **a** and **b**, in hours and minutes.

10 A man walked from his home to the next village, a distance of 15 km. It took him 2 hours and 45 minutes.

    a Find his average speed in km/h.

    Give your answer correct to 1 decimal place.

On the way back, he had to bring his father with him. The father could only walk at an average speed of 4.2 km/h.

    b How long did it take them to return to the man's home?

    Give your answer to the nearest minute.

11 There is a gap of T seconds between a person seeing a flash of lightning and hearing the thunder clap that follows. This time, T, is directly proportional to the distance, D kilometres, that the person is from the centre of the storm.

When the centre of the storm is 3 km away, the time gap is 9 seconds.

    a When you are 7 km away, find the time gap between seeing the lightning and first hearing the thunder.

    b How far away would you be if there was a time gap of 8 seconds?

12 Kirsty buys a bag of food for her rabbit.

During the first week, the rabbit eats $\frac{1}{4}$ of the food.

During the second week, the rabbit eats $\frac{2}{5}$ of the remaining food.

What fraction of the food is left after the second week?

3 Algebra

Revise 3.1 Basic algebra

Using letters for numbers

In algebra, a letter stands for an unknown number.

It is called a **variable** because it can take different values.

$4x + 2x + 5x - 3x$ is an **expression** and $4x$, $+2x$, $+5x$, $-3x$ are the **terms** of the expression.

To **simplify** the expression, add and subtract the number of xs.

$$4x + 2x + 5x - 3x = 8x$$

When the expression contains more than one variable, there will be **like terms** and **unlike terms**.

In the expression $2p + 4q - p + q - 2q$,

$2p$ and $+4q$ are unlike terms,

$2p$ and $-p$ are like terms and can be simplified to p, which you write as just p,

$+ 4q + q - 2q$ are like terms and can be simplified to $+3q$.

$$2p + 4q - p + q - 2q = p + 3q$$

Exam tip

The sign in front of each term 'belongs' to that term and stays with it when you collect like terms.

Expressing basic arithmetic processes algebraically

$3 \times a$ is written as $3a$. You do not show the multiplication sign.

$a \times b$ is written as ab.

This is the same as ba because 5×3 is the same as 3×5.

$a \times a$ is written as a^2.

$a \times a \times a$ is written as a^3.

Exam tip

Be careful not to confuse a^2 with $2a$.
a^2 means $a \times a$ but $2a$ means $a + a$.

In the expression $\quad 3a^2 + 2a - ab + 5a - a^2 + 4ba,$

$\quad\quad 3a^2$ and $-a^2 \quad$ are like terms and can be simplified to $2a^2$

$\quad\quad +2a$ and $+5a \quad$ are like terms and can be simplified to $+7a$

$\quad\quad -ab$ and $+4ba$ are like terms and can be simplified to $+3ab$

$$\quad\quad 3a^2 + 2a - ab + 5a - a^2 + 4ba = 2a^2 + 7a + 3ab$$

Substitution

Replacing the letters in an expression with numbers to find its value is called **substitution**.

If you are given the expression $7x - 4y$, you can substitute numbers for x and y to find its value.

If $x = 5$ and $y = -2$, then $7x - 4y = (7 \times 5) - (4 \times -2)$

$$= 35 - (-8)$$
$$= 35 + 8$$
$$= 43$$

Exam tip

Use brackets to help you to get the signs right.

Using formulae

A **formula** can be written in words or in symbols.

The formula for the area of a triangle can be written as:

$\quad$ Area equals half the base multiplied by the height.

Using A for the area, b for the base and h for the height, this can be written in symbols as:

$\quad A = \frac{1}{2}bh$

If you know the value of b and of h, you can then work out the area.

For example, if $b = 6.4\,\text{cm}$ and $h = 5\,\text{cm}$, then $A = \frac{1}{2} \times 6.4 \times 5 = 16\,\text{cm}^2$.

Worked example

Substitution

$x = 0.6$ and $y = -0.5$

Find the value of :

a $\;3x + 4y$ $\qquad\qquad$ **b** $\;2x^2 - y^2$ $\qquad\qquad$ **c** $\;\dfrac{5x}{4y}$

Solution

Start by writing down the expression, and then put in the numbers ($x = 0.6$, $y = -0.5$).

a $3x + 4y = (3 \times 0.6) + (4 \times -0.5)$

$\qquad\qquad = 1.8 + (-2)$

$\qquad\qquad = -0.2$

b $2x^2 - y^2 = (2 \times 0.6 \times 0.6) - (-0.5 \times -0.5)$

$\qquad\qquad\quad = 0.72 - (0.25)$

$\qquad\qquad\quad = 0.47$

c $\dfrac{5x}{4y} = \dfrac{5 \times 0.6}{4 \times -0.5}$

$\qquad = \dfrac{3}{-2}$

$\qquad = -1.5$

Revise 3.2 More algebra

Expanding brackets

To **expand** a bracket, you multiply each term inside the bracket by the term outside the bracket.

$\quad 2p(p - 4) = 2p \times p + 2p \times -4$

$\qquad\qquad\quad = 2p^2 - 8p$

If an expression has more than one bracket, it may contain like terms.

$\quad 2p(p - 4) + 5(p - 3) = 2p^2 - 8p + 5p - 15$

$\qquad\qquad\qquad\qquad\quad = 2p^2 - 3p - 15$

> **Exam tip**
>
> If an exam question says 'expand and simplify' there will be like terms to collect up.

Indices

x^2 means $x \times x$.

ab^2 means $a \times b \times b$.

$n^a \times n^b = n^{a+b}$

$n^a \div n^b = n^{a-b}$

$(n^a)^b = n^{ab}$

So $(5a^3)^2 \div 2a^4 = 25a^6 \div 2a^4 = 12\frac{1}{2}a^2$

Factorising expressions

To **factorise** an expression, you do the opposite of expanding a bracket.

You will be told to factorise an expression, such as $3q^2 + 2q$.

The two terms in this expression have a **common factor**, q.

$$3q^2 + 2q = q(3q + 2)$$

Exam tip

After factorising, multiply out again to check your answer.

Constructing simple expressions

1 'Joe thinks of a number, doubles it and adds 9.'

Let the number be x.

This can be written in algebra as '$2x + 9$'.

2 'Jake is two years older than Paul and George is three times as old as Jake'.

Let Paul's age be p years.

Jake's age can be written as $(p + 2)$ years and George's age as $3(p + 2)$ years.

Exam tip

In the exam, you will probably be told which letter to use for the unknown number.

Solving linear equations

You will be asked to **solve** an equation to find the value of the **unknown** (for example, x).

You do this by reversing the operations, always doing the same to both sides of the equation.

1 In the equation $x - 6 = 2$, you add 6 to both sides to get $x = 8$.

2 In the equation $\frac{y}{5} = 3$, you multiply both sides by 5 to get $y = 15$.

If the equation has more than one operation, you have to think of the order of operations.

3 In the equation $8a + 1 = 25$, there are two operations: 'multiply a by 8 and then add 1'.

The second operation 'add 1' is the first one you reverse to solve the equation.

$$8a + 1 = 25$$

Subtract 1 from both sides: $8a = 24$

Divide both sides by 8: $a = 3$

4 You may have to find the equation first.

'Joe thinks of a number, doubles it and adds 9. His answer is 23.'

This can be written as the equation

$$2x + 9 = 23.$$

Exam tip

- It is usually a good idea to check your answer by substituting it back into the original equation.
- But if it is a very odd fraction such as $\frac{11}{17}$, (or a lengthy decimal) don't substitute!
- Instead, check your working as you may have made a mistake.

Changing the subject of a formula

The subject of a formula is the letter at the start of the formula, before the equals sign.

Changing the subject of (or **transforming**) the formula uses the same steps as for solving an equation.

The formula for the area of a triangle, $A = \frac{1}{2}bh$, can be transformed to become a formula to find the height.

Multiply both sides by 2: $2A = bh$

Divide both sides by b: $\frac{2A}{b} = h$

Write the answer in the form '$h = \ldots$' $h = \frac{2A}{b}$

Solving equations with the unknown on both sides

You have to collect all the terms in x (or whichever letter is used) on one side of the equation.

You have to collect all the other terms on the other side.

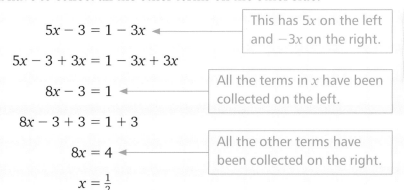

$$5x - 3 = 1 - 3x$$

This has $5x$ on the left and $-3x$ on the right.

$$5x - 3 + 3x = 1 - 3x + 3x$$

$$8x - 3 = 1$$

All the terms in x have been collected on the left.

$$8x - 3 + 3 = 1 + 3$$

$$8x = 4$$

All the other terms have been collected on the right.

$$x = \tfrac{1}{2}$$

Exam tip

Take great care with the signs in front of the terms.

Equations with brackets

Your first step is to remove the bracket, usually by multiplying it out.

Then solve the equation by doing the same to both sides.

For example, to solve the equation

$$4(y - 3) = 3y - 8$$

start by multiplying out $4(y - 3)$

$$4y - 12 = 3y - 8$$

then collect up terms to get

$$y = 4$$

Exam tip

Don't forget to multiply the second term in the bracket by the term in front of the bracket.

The worked example opposite shows how you can sometimes start by dividing both sides.

Equations with fractions

To solve an equation containing a fraction, you have to multiply both sides by the **denominator**.

Starting with $\dfrac{x}{3} = 12$

Multiply both sides by 3 $\quad x = 36$

If there is more than one fraction, multiply by the **lowest common denominator**.

Starting with $\quad \dfrac{a}{4} = 10 - \dfrac{a}{6}$ the lowest common denominator of 4 and 6 is 12.

Multiply both sides by 12 $\quad 12 \times \dfrac{a}{4} = 12 \times 10 - 12 \times \dfrac{a}{6}$

$$3a = 120 - 2a$$
$$5a = 120$$
$$a = 24$$

If there are two terms on top of the fraction, put brackets round them before you multiply, as shown in the worked example opposite.

Worked examples

Equations with brackets

Solve the equation $\quad 5(x - 2) = 30$

Solution

Multiply out the bracket $\quad 5x - 10 = 30$

Add 10 to both sides $\quad 5x = 40$

Divide by 5 $\quad x = 8$

Alternative solution

Divide both sides by 5 $\quad \dfrac{\overset{1}{\cancel{5}}(x-2)}{\cancel{5}^1} = \dfrac{\cancel{30}^6}{\cancel{5}^1}$

$$x - 2 = 6$$
$$x = 8$$

Equations with fractions

Solve the equation $\dfrac{2x+5}{3} - \dfrac{6-x}{2} = 1$

Solution

Put brackets round the terms on top of the fractions.

$$\frac{(2x+5)}{3} - \frac{(6-x)}{2} = 1$$

Multiply by the lowest common denominator, 6.

$$^{2}\cancel{6} \times \frac{(2x+5)}{\cancel{3}^{1}} - ^{3}\cancel{6} \times \frac{(6-x)}{\cancel{2}^{1}} = 6 \times 1$$

$$2(2x+5) - 3(6-x) = 6$$

$$4x + 10 - 18 + 3x = 6 \qquad \boxed{-3 \times -x = +3x}$$

$$7x - 8 = 6$$

$$7x = 14$$

$$x = 2$$

Revise 3.3 Sequences

The rules of a sequence

A **sequence** is a set of numbers or patterns with a given **rule** or pattern, e.g. 1, 4, 9, 16, 25.

Each number in the sequence is called a **term**.

The sequences can be shown using patterns or diagrams.

If a sequence goes on for ever, it is called an **infinite** sequence.

This is shown by a series of dots, e.g. 3, 6, 9, 12, … .

A rule can be written in two different ways: as a **term-to-term rule** or using a formula for the *n*th **term**.

Term-to-term rule

A term-to-term rule explains how you get from one term to the next in the sequence.

The rule could be 'divide by 2' or 'subtract 5'.

It could also be a combination of two parts, such as 'divide by 4 and then add on 3'.
Be careful as order matters.

Each term is compared to the next term.

If you were asked for the 100th term, you would need to know the 98th, 97th, and so on.

This could take a long time.

Formula for the nth term

A **position-to-term rule** is a formula for any number in a sequence.

For example, a sequence has an nth term of $3n - 1$.

Then the first term (when $n = 1$) is $3 \times 1 - 1 = 2$.

The second term (when ($n = 2$) is $3 \times 2 - 1 = 5$.

The third, fourth and fifth terms are $3 \times 3 - 1 = 8$, $3 \times 4 - 1 = 11$, and $3 \times 5 - 1 = 14$.

So the sequence starts   2   5   8   11   14   ...

The 100th term is $3 \times 100 - 1 = 299$.

This is an **arithmetic sequence**. Arithmetic sequences have a common difference between terms.

In this sequence, the common difference is 3, as the terms increase by 3 each time.

The common difference is 3 because of the $3n$ in the rule for the nth term.

The sequence with nth term of $3n$ is   3   6   9   12   ...   or the three times table.

So 2, 5, 8, 11, ... has terms which are one less than the three times table, or $3n - 1$.

To find the nth term of the sequence

6   10   14   18   22   ...

First find the common difference, which is 4.

So the nth term contains $4n$.

$4n$ is the nth term of the four times table,   4   8   12   16   ...

The sequence   6   10   14   18   22   ...   has terms which are 2 more than the four times table, so the nth term is $4n + 2$

So an arithmetic sequence with a common difference of a has an nth term of $an + k$.

You can find the value of k by comparing a and the first term.

The sequence   9   7   5   3   ...   has a common difference of -2, so the nth term is $-2n + k$.

The first term, 9, is 11 more than -2, so $k = 11$, and the nth term is $-2n + 11$.

Other common sequences

You should also be able to recognise the following sequences:

1, 4, 9, 16, 25, ...	Squares
1, 8, 27, 64, 125, 216, ...	Cubes
1, 2, 4, 8, 16, ...	The next term is double the previous term. It is also powers of 2.
$1, \frac{1}{2}, \frac{1}{3}, \frac{1}{4}, ...$	Reciprocals
1, 3, 6, 10, 15, ...	Triangular numbers
1, 1, 2, 3, 5, 8, ...	The Fibonacci sequence, where each term is the sum of the previous two terms

Finding the nth term

a Find the nth term of the sequence:

  3   7   11   15   19   ...

b Find the value of the hundredth term.

c Using your previous answers, find the value of the hundredth term of this sequence:

  2   6   10   14   18   ...

Solution

a The nth term is found by comparing the term to its position in the sequence: 1st, 2nd, 3rd, etc.

1st	2nd	3rd	4th	5th
3	7	11	15	19

  +4   +4   +4   +4

When finding this nth term, it is still useful to know the difference between the terms of the sequence.

The above diagram shows that the common difference between the terms is 4. This means that there is a $4n$ in the nth term.

n	1	2	3	4
Sequence	3	7	11	15
4n	4 $^{-1}$	8 $^{-1}$	12 $^{-1}$	16 $^{-1}$

The first term, 3, is 1 less than the common difference of 4.

So the nth term of the sequence is $4n - 1$.

b To find the value of the 100th term, replace n by 100 in the formula for the nth term:

$$\text{value of 100th term} = 4 \times 100 - 1$$
$$= 400 - 1$$
$$= 399$$

c Every number in the new sequence is one less than the corresponding number in the previous sequence.

So the value of the 100th term is $399 - 1 = 398$.

Comparing sequences

The nth term of the sequence:

  3   4   7   12   19   ...

is $(n - 1)^2 + 3$.

Write down the formula for the nth term of the sequence:

  6   9   14   21   30   ...

Simplify your answer.

Solution

$$3, \quad 4, \quad 7, \quad 12, \quad 19, \quad \dots$$
$$6, \quad 9, \quad 14, \quad 21, \quad 30, \quad \dots$$

Comparing the sequences

$$\begin{array}{ccccc} 3 & 4 & 7 & 12 & 19 \\ +3\downarrow & +5\downarrow & +7\downarrow & +9\downarrow & +11\downarrow \\ 6 & 9 & 14 & 21 & 30 \end{array}$$

The differences are 3, 5, 7, 9, 11, … .

Each of these numbers in the sequence of differences increases by 2, so there is a $2n$ in the formula.

The nth term of the sequence of differences is $2n + 1$.

The nth term for the sequence 6, 9, 14, 21, 30, ... is $(n - 1)^2 + 3 + 2n + 1$

This simplifies to $n^2 - 2n + 1 + 3 + 2n + 1 = n^2 + 5$.

Check

When $n = 1$, 1st term is $1^2 + 5 = 6$.

When $n = 2$, 2nd term is $2^2 + 5 = 9$, and so on.

Patterns in sequences

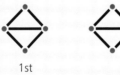 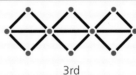

| 1st diagram | 2nd diagram | 3rd diagram |

a Copy and complete the table showing the total number of lines and the number of dots in each pattern:

Diagram	1st	2nd	3rd	4th	5th
Lines	5	10	15		
Dots	4	7			

b Find the nth term for: **i** the number of lines used   **ii** the number of dots used.

c From your previous answers, show that the nth term for the total number of lines and dots is $8n + 1$.

d Which diagram has a total number of 137 dots and lines?

Solution

a

Diagram	1st	2nd	3rd	4th	5th
Lines	5	10	15	**20**	**25**
Dots	4	7	**10**	**13**	**16**

b   **i** The numbers in the second row, labelled lines, are exactly 5 times the diagram numbers.

So the nth term of the sequence for the number of lines is $5n$.

You could also obtain this answer by noticing that the common difference between the terms of the sequence is always 5.

ii Comparing each term with the next, the common difference is 3.

This means that there is a $3n$ in the nth term.

Diagram	1st	2nd	3rd	4th	5th
Dots	4	7	10	13	16
3n	3 +1	6 +1	9 +1	12 +1	15 +1

To return to the original sequence from the $3n$ row, you need to add 1 to each number.

The nth term of the sequence for the number of dots is $3n + 1$.

c nth term for lines $= 5n$

nth term for dots $= 3n + 1$

So adding these expressions gives:

nth term for total number of lines and dots $= 8n + 1$

Diagram	1st	2nd	3rd	4th	5th
Lines	5	10	15	20	25
Dots	4	7	10	13	16
Lines + dots	9	17	25	33	41

d The number of lines and dots in the nth diagram $= 8n + 1$. This is equal to 137.

So $8n + 1 = 137$

$8n = 137 - 1$ ←———————————— Subtract 1 from each side.

$8n = 136$

$n = \dfrac{136}{8}$

$n = 17$

The 17th diagram has a total of 137 lines and dots.

Revise 3.4 Functions

Functions

A **function** is a mapping where each input maps to exactly one output.

All the numbers that can be inputs are called the **domain**.

The numbers that can be fed out make up the **range**.

Function notation

The function f such that f: $x \rightarrow 11 - 2x$, tells us that the number, x, is multiplied by 2 and then subtracted from 11.

It may also be written as $f(x) = 11 - 2x$

The equation $y = 11 - 2x$ describes the same operations.

For this function, $f(4) = 11 - 2 \times 4 = 3$ and

$f(-1) = 11 - 2 \times -1 = 13$

> **Exam tip**
>
> Remember BIDMAS when you substitute a value for x in the function.

Composite functions

gf is an example of a **composite function**.

gf means 'use function f first, followed by function g'.

If $f(x) = 6x$ and $g(x) = 2x + 9$

$$gf(-1) = g(-6)$$
$$= (2 \times -6) + 9 = -3$$

gf(x) is not the same as fg(x).

$$fg(-1) = f(2 \times -1 + 9)$$
$$= f(7) = 42$$

Inverse functions

f^{-1} is the **inverse** function that reverses the processes of f.

If $y = f(x)$, then $f^{-1}(y) = x$.

To find f^{-1}, write $f(x) = ...$ as $y = ...$ For example, $f(x) = 3x - 2$ is written as $y = 3x - 2$

Rearrange the equation to make x the subject $y + 2 = 3x$, so $x = \dfrac{y + 2}{3}$

Rewrite as a function of x $f^{-1}(y) = \dfrac{y + 2}{3}$, so $f^{-1}(x) = \dfrac{x + 2}{3}$,

To check your answer, use a number for x and find $f(x)$.

Then put the result number into the function $f^{-1}(x)$ and you should get back to your starting number.

Worked example

Functions

$f(x) = \dfrac{1}{x - 2}$ and $g(x) = 4x$

a Write down a value of x that cannot be in any domain of f.

b Find the value of x when $f(x) = 10$.

c Express the function fg in the form $fg(x) = ...$

d Find $f^{-1}(x)$.

e Find the value of $gf^{-1}(10)$.

Solution

a $x = 2$ cannot be in the domain because $f(x)$ is not defined, as it equals $\dfrac{1}{0}$

b $\dfrac{1}{x - 2} = 10$

$$1 = 10(x - 2)$$
$$1 = 10x - 20$$
$$21 = 10x$$
$$x = 2.1$$

c $fg(x) = f(4x)$

$$= \frac{1}{4x - 2}$$

d To find the inverse function, write $f(x)$ as $y = \dfrac{1}{x - 2}$

Make x the subject of the formula: $y(x - 2) = 1$

$$xy - 2y = 1$$

$$xy = 1 + 2y$$

$$x = \frac{1 + 2y}{y}$$

The inverse function is $f^{-1}(x) = \dfrac{1 + 2x}{x}$ ⟵ Remember to put x back in instead of y.

e $f^{-1}(10) = \dfrac{1 + 2 \times 10}{10} = 2.1$

$gf^{-1}(10) = g(2.1) = 8.4$

Practise 3.1 – 3.4

1 Simplify:

   a $x + 4y - 2y + 5x$ **b** $2pq - p^2 + 5qp + 3p^2$ **c** $m^3 - m - 3m + 5 - m^3$

2 $a = -1$ and $b = -7$

  Find the value of: **a** $a^2 + b^2$ **b** $a^3 - b$.

3 Use the formula $I = \dfrac{PRT}{100}$ to find I when $P = 2400$, $R = 2.25$ and $T = 3$.

4 Multiply out and simplify $6(x - 1) - 2(3 + x)$.

5 Factorise:

   a $12x + 4$ **b** $6uv - 2v$

6 A melon costs $\$x$ and an orange costs $\$y$ dollars.

  Martina buys 4 melons and 15 oranges.

  Write down an expression in x and y for the total cost.

7 Solve these equations.

   a $4p + 11 = 9$ **b** $\dfrac{5q}{8} = 3$ **c** $9 = 4(t - 1)$

8 A taxi fare is worked out as a fixed charge of $12 plus $1.25 per kilometre.

Roberto pays $20.75 for his journey of x kilometres.

Write down an equation in x and solve it to find how far Roberto travelled.

9 Make a the subject of the formula $P = 2a + 2b$

10 Solve these equations.

a $9x + 2 = 4(2x - 1)$

b $\dfrac{2y + 7}{4} = 3$

c $\dfrac{m + 3}{2} - \dfrac{m - 3}{4} = 4$

11 $f(x) = x^2 + 1$ and $g(x) = 5 - x$

a Find the value of $f(-6)$.

b Show that $g^{-1}(x) = g(x)$.

c Find $fg(4)$.

d Find $gf(x)$.

e Explain why 0 cannot be a member of any range of f.

12 a Write down the first five terms of each of these sequences:

  i 1st term = 7, rule = +6

  ii 1st term = 9, rule = −4

  iii 1st term = 1, rule = ×2, then +1.

b The nth term of a sequence is $\dfrac{n}{n^2 + 1}$.

Write down the first five terms of the sequence.

13 a **i** Write down the next two terms in the sequence: 15   9   3   −3   …

  ii Explain how you worked out your answers.

  iii Find an expression for the nth term of the sequence.

b Write down an expression for the nth term of this sequence: 3   9   15   21   27   …

c Find the sum of:

  i the first term of each sequence.

  ii the second term of each sequence.

d Add the expressions for the nth terms of the two sequences.

14 Here is a sequence of patterns made using short lines and crosses.

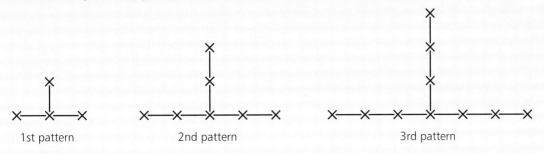

1st pattern   2nd pattern   3rd pattern

a Copy and complete the table below:

Pattern	1st	2nd	3rd	4th	5th
Lines	3	6			
Crosses	4	7			

b For the 7th pattern, find the number of:

   i lines   **ii** crosses.

c For the nth pattern, find an expression for the number of:

   i lines   **ii** crosses.

d How many crosses are in the 50th pattern?

e How many lines are there in the pattern with 76 crosses?

15 The formula for the nth term of the sequence:

$$1\tfrac{3}{5}, \quad 3, \quad 4\tfrac{4}{5}, \quad 7, \quad ...$$

is $\dfrac{(n + 1)(n + 3)}{k}$, where k is an integer.

a Find the value of k.

b Test your formula when $n = 3$. Show your working.

c Find the 74th term in the sequence.

4 Measures and mensuration

Learning outcomes

After this chapter you should be able to:

- use and convert units of mass, length, area, volume and capacity in practical problems
- carry out calculations involving perimeters and areas of rectangles, triangles, parallelograms and trapezia
- carry out calculations involving the circumference and area of a circle
- draw and recognise the nets of solids
- carry out calculations involving the surface area of cuboids, cylinders, prisms and other solids
- carry out calculations involving the volume of cuboids, prisms and cylinders
- calculate the length of an arc
- calculate the area of a sector
- calculate the surface area and volume of spheres, pyramids and cones from given formulae.

Revise 4.1 Measures

You must know the metric units and **conversion factors** below.

To convert to a smaller unit, multiply by the conversion factor (so there are more of them).

To convert to a larger unit, divide by the conversion factor (so there are fewer of them).

Mass

1 tonne = 1000 kilograms (1 t = 1000 kg)

1 kilogram = 1000 grams (1 kg = 1000 g)

1 gram = 1000 milligrams (1 g = 1000 mg)

Length

1 kilometre = 1000 metres (1 km = 1000 m)

1 metre = 1000 millimetres (1 m = 1000 mm)

1 metre = 100 centimetres (1 m = 100 cm)

1 centimetre = 10 millimetres (1 cm = 10 mm)

> Remember kilo means 1000, milli means $\frac{1}{1000}$ and centi means $\frac{1}{100}$.

Capacity

1 litre = 1000 millilitres (1 l = 1000 ml)

1 litre = 100 centilitres (1 l = 100 cl)

1 centilitre = 10 millilitres (1 cl = 10 ml)

> Note also that 1 ml = 1 cm³ so 1 l = 1000 cm³ and 1 m³ = 1000 l.

Converting units of area and volume

Remember that the conversion factors for area and volume are not the same as those for length.

For example, $1\,m^2 = 100^2\,cm^2 = 10\,000\,cm^2$ and $1\,m^3 = 100^3\,cm^3 = 1\,000\,000\,cm^3$.

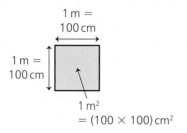

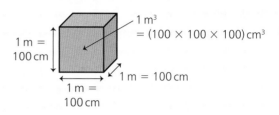

Worked example

Metric units

The area of a lake on a map is $8\,cm^2$.

The actual area of the lake is 625 million times the area of the lake on the map.

Find the actual area of the lake in km^2.

Solution

Actual area of lake $= 625\,000\,000 \times 8\,cm^2 = 5\,000\,000\,000\,cm^2$

$= 5\,000\,000\,000 \div 10\,000 = 500\,000\,m^2$ $\boxed{1\,m^2 = 100^2\,cm^2 = 10\,000\,cm^2}$

$= 500\,000 \div 1\,000\,000 = 0.5\,km^2$ $\boxed{1\,km^2 = 1000^2\,m^2 = 1\,000\,000\,m^2}$

> **Exam tip**
>
> To convert to a smaller unit, multiply by the conversion factor.
> To convert to a larger unit, divide by the conversion factor.

 Revise 4.2 Mensuration: perimeter and area

Perimeter

The **perimeter** of any shape is the total length of its sides.

For example, the perimeter of a rectangle

    $=$ length $+$ width $+$ length $+$ width or 2(length $+$ width).

In the metric system, perimeters are measured in mm, cm, m or km.

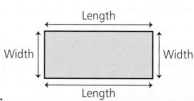

Area

Area is the amount of space inside a shape.

In the metric system, areas are measured in mm², cm², m² or km².

Area formulae

- Area of a rectangle = length × width or $A = lw$

- Area of a parallelogram = base × perpendicular height

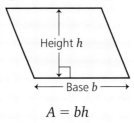

$$A = bh$$

- Area of a triangle = $\frac{1}{2}$ × base × perpendicular height

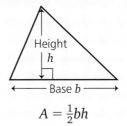

$$A = \frac{1}{2}bh$$

> Remember the height must be perpendicular to the base.

- Area of a trapezium

  = $\frac{1}{2}$ × sum of parallel sides × perpendicular height

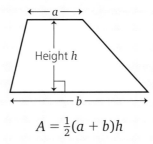

$$A = \frac{1}{2}(a + b)h$$

Circles

Length of the circumference of a circle, $C = \pi \times$ diameter $= \pi d = 2\pi r$.

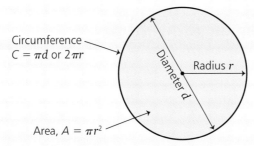

> The diameter is twice as long as the radius $d = 2r$.

Area of a circle, $A = \pi \times$ radius × radius $= \pi r^2$.

Worked examples

Perimeter and area of 2-D shapes

The diagram shows a trapezium *ABCD* with *AD* = *BC* and a square *ABXY*.

a Write the perimeter of *ABXY* as a fraction of the perimeter of *ABCD*, giving your answer in its simplest form.

b Write the area of *ABXY* as a percentage of the area of *ABCD*.

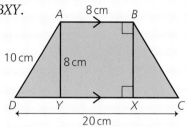

Solution

a Perimeter of *ABXY* = 32 cm

Perimeter of *ABCD* = 10 + 8 + 10 + 20 = 48 cm

Perimeter of *ABXY* as a fraction of the perimeter of *ABCD* = $\frac{32}{48}$ = $\frac{2}{3}$ after cancelling

b Area of *ABXY* = 8 × 8 = 64 cm² ◄—————— *ABXY* is a square of side 8 cm.

Area of *ABCD* = $\frac{1}{2}$ × (8 + 20) × 8

> Area of a trapezium
> = $\frac{1}{2}$ × sum of parallel sides
> × perpendicular height

$\qquad\qquad$ = $\frac{1}{2}$ × 28 × 8

$\qquad\qquad$ = 112 cm²

> You can work this out by calculating 14 × 8 or 28 × 4 or $\frac{1}{2}$ of (28 × 8).

Area of *ABXY* as a percentage of the area of *ABCD* = $\frac{64}{112}$ × 100% = 57.1% (to 1 d.p.)

Composite shape

A triangular hole is cut from a circular card.

Calculate the area of the shaded part.

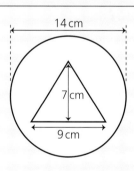

Solution

Area of circle = π × 7² = 153.9... cm² | Area of circle = πr^2

Area of triangle = $\frac{1}{2}$ × 9 × 7 | Area of a triangle = $\frac{1}{2}$ × base × perpendicular height

$\qquad\qquad$ = $\frac{1}{2}$ × 63 = 31.5 cm²

Shaded area = 153.9... − 31.5

$\qquad\qquad$ = 122.4... = 122 cm² (to 3 s.f.)

> **Exam tip**
>
> Work as accurately as you can.
> Use the calculator's memory
> if necessary. Rounding values
> too soon may lose marks.

Revise 4.3 Mensuration: volume and surface area

Volume

Volume is the amount of space inside a 3-D shape.

In the metric system, volume is measured in mm^3, cm^3, m^3 or km^3.

A **prism** is a solid with the same cross-section throughout its length.

Volume of a prism = area of cross-section × length

A **cuboid** is a type of prism. A **cylinder** also has a constant circular cross-section.

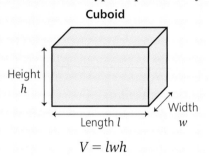
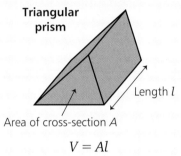
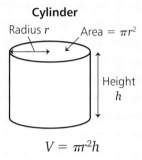

Cuboid

Height h

Length l

Width w

$V = lwh$

Triangular prism

Length l

Area of cross-section A

$V = Al$

Cylinder

Radius r Area $= \pi r^2$

Height h

$V = \pi r^2 h$

Volume of a pyramid or cone = $\frac{1}{3}$ base area × perpendicular height

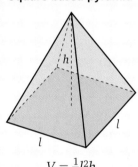

Square-based pyramid

h

l

l

$V = \frac{1}{3}l^2h$

Cone

h l

r

$V = \frac{1}{3}\pi r^2 h$

Exam tip

Remember to put all dimensions into the same units before working out the area or volume of a shape.

Volume of a sphere $= \frac{4}{3}\pi r^3$

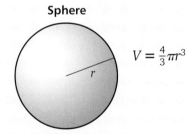

Sphere

r

$V = \frac{4}{3}\pi r^3$

The volume of a container is sometimes called its **capacity**.

Nets and surface area

A face is part of the surface of a solid – it is enclosed by edges.

An edge is a line where 2 faces meet.

A vertex is a point where 3 or more edges meet.

A cuboid has 6 **faces**, 12 **edges** and 8 **vertices**.

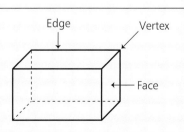

Edge   Vertex

Face

The **surface area** of a cube or cuboid is the total area of its 6 faces.

The diagram shows a **net** of the cuboid.

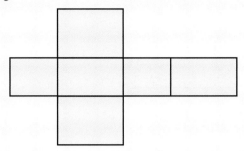

> Note there are other ways of arranging the faces in the net. For example:

The net of a cylinder consists of two circles and a rectangle.

The length of the rectangle is equal to the circumference of the circle.

The area of the curved surface is $2\pi rh$.

The total surface area $= 2\pi rh + 2\pi r^2$, or $2\pi r(h + r)$.

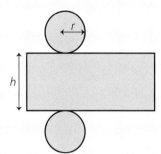

Surface area of a sphere, $A = 4\pi r^2$

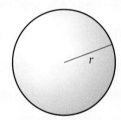

Curved surface area of a cone of radius r and slant height l is

$A = \pi rl$

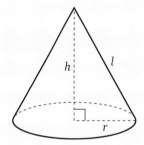

Worked examples

Nets and surface area

A cylindrical can has diameter 7.6 cm and height 11.2 cm.

a Draw a sketch of the net of this can.

b Work out the total surface area of the can.

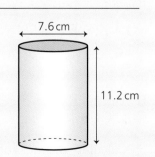

7.6 cm

11.2 cm

Solution

a The diagram shows the net of the can.

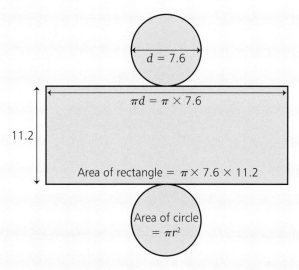

b The radius of each circle $= 7.6 \div 2 = 3.8\,\text{cm}$

The area of each circle $= \pi r^2 = \pi \times 3.8 \times 3.8 = 45.364\ldots$ ← Put this value into your calculator's memory to use later.

The length of the rectangle $= \pi \times 7.6$

The area of the rectangle $= \pi \times 7.6 \times 11.2 = 267.412\ldots$

Total surface area of the cylinder $= 267.412\ldots + 2 \times 45.364\ldots$ ← Carry on the working with the value from your calculator's memory.

$= 358\,\text{cm}^2$ (to the nearest cm^2)

Exam tip

Remember to work as accurately as you can and only round your answer at the end of the calculation.

Volume and mass

The diagram shows a block of stone of length 1.2 metres.

The cross-section is a rectangle with a trapezium on top.

a Calculate:

   i the area of the cross-section

   ii the volume of the block of stone, giving your answer in cubic centimetres.

b The mass of 1 cubic centimetre of the stone is 5 grams.

Calculate the mass of the block. Give your answer in kilograms.

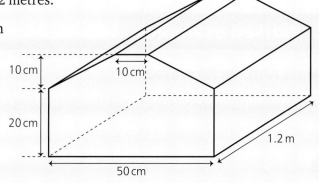

Solution

a   i Area of rectangle = $50 \times 20 = 1000 \text{ cm}^2$

> **Area of a trapezium**
> $= \frac{1}{2} \times$ sum of parallel sides $\times$ perpendicular height

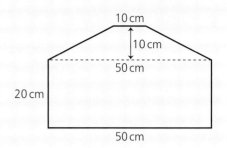

Area of trapezium $= \frac{1}{2} \times (10 + 50) \times 10$

$\qquad\qquad\qquad = \frac{1}{2} \times 60 \times 10 = 300 \text{ cm}^2$

Area of cross-section $= 1000 + 300 = 1300 \text{ cm}^2$

Cross-section

Exam tip

Write all dimensions in the same units before using an area or volume formula.

ii The length of the block of stone = 1.2 m

$\qquad\qquad\qquad\qquad = 1.2 \times 100 = 120 \text{ cm}$

> 1 m = 100 cm

Volume of the block of stone = 1300×120

$\qquad\qquad\qquad\qquad = 156\,000 \text{ cm}^3$

> **Volume of a prism**
> = area of cross-section $\times$ length

b   The mass of the block of stone = $156\,000 \times 5 \text{ g} = 780\,000 \text{ g}$

$\qquad\qquad\qquad\qquad = 780\,000 \div 1000 = 780 \text{ kg}$

> 1 kg = 1000 g

Cone and cylinder

A cone and a cylinder both have a radius of 5 cm.

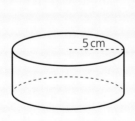
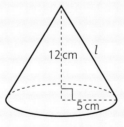

The height of the cone is 12 cm.

The surface area of the cone and the cylinder are equal.

Calculate the volume of:

a   the cone,

b   the cylinder,

leaving your answers in terms of π.

Solution

a Volume of the cone $= \frac{1}{3}\pi r^2 h$

$$= \frac{1}{3} \times \pi \times 5^2 \times 12$$

$$= 100\pi \, \text{cm}^3$$

b Volume of the cylinder $= \pi r^2 h$

$r = 5$ cm but the height, h, is unknown.

Using surface area of cone = surface area of cylinder

$$\pi r l + \pi r^2 = 2\pi r h + 2\pi r^2$$

$$l + r = 2h + 2r \quad \longleftarrow \boxed{\text{Dividing every term by } \pi r.}$$

$$l - r = 2h$$

$$\frac{l - r}{2} = h$$

By Pythagoras,

$$l^2 = 12^2 + 5^2$$

$$l^2 = 144 + 25 = 169$$

$$l = 13$$

$$h = \frac{l - r}{2}$$

$$h = \frac{13 - 5}{2} = 4$$

Volume of the cylinder $= \pi r^2 h = \pi \times 5^2 \times 4 = 100\pi \, \text{cm}^3$

> A cylinder has 2 circular faces + a curved surface:
>
> $C = 2\pi r$
>
> Area of curved surface $= 2\pi r h$ $\bigg| h$

Hemisphere

The volume of a hemisphere is $144\pi \, \text{cm}^3$.

Find the total surface area of the hemisphere, giving your answer in terms of π.

Solution

For a hemisphere, $V = \frac{2}{3}\pi r^3$

$$\frac{2}{3}\pi r^3 = 144\pi$$

$$r^3 = \frac{3 \times 144}{2} = 216$$

$$r = \sqrt[3]{216} = 6 \, \text{cm}$$

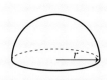

Total surface area of the hemisphere

$= $ curved surface area $+$ area of circular base

$$= 2\pi r^2 + \pi r^2 = 3\pi r^2$$

$$= 3\pi \times 6^2$$

$$= 108\pi \, \text{cm}^2$$

Exam tip

You will be given these formulae in the examination:

- a sphere of radius r has surface area $A = 4\pi r^2$ and volume $V = \frac{4}{3}\pi r^3$
- a cone of radius r, height h and slant height l has a curved surface area $A = \pi rl$ and volume $V = \frac{1}{3}\pi r^2 h$.

Revise 4.4 Arc lengths and sector areas

Length of an arc

An **arc** is part of the circumference of a circle.

If the angle at the centre is $\theta°$, then

length of arc $= \dfrac{\theta}{360} \times$ circumference

$\qquad\qquad = \dfrac{\theta}{360} \times 2\pi r$ or $\dfrac{\theta}{360} \times \pi d$

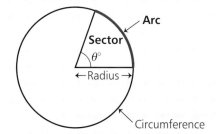

Area of a sector

A region bounded by two radii and an arc is a **sector**.

If the angle at the centre is $\theta°$, then

area of sector $= \dfrac{\theta}{360} \times$ area of circle

$\qquad\qquad = \dfrac{\theta}{360} \times \pi r^2$

Exam tip

It is useful to leave your answers in terms of π until the end of the question.

Worked example

Arc and sector

A shape consists of a square of side 6 cm and a sector of a circle as shown.

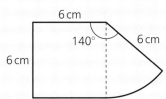

Calculate:

a the area of the shape

b the perimeter of the shape.

Solution

a   Area of the square $= 6 \times 6 = 36 \, \text{cm}^2$

Area of the sector $= \dfrac{50}{360} \times \pi \times 6^2$

$= 15.7... \, \text{cm}^2$

Total area of the shape $= 15.7... + 36 = 51.7 \, \text{cm}^2$ (to 1 d.p.)

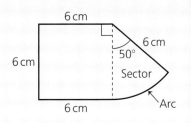

b The perimeter consists of 4 sides of 6 cm + the arc

Perimeter of the shape $= 24 + \dfrac{50}{360} \times \pi \times 12$

$= 24 + 5.23...$

$= 29.2 \, \text{cm}$ (to 1 d.p.)

Practise 4.1 – 4.4

1 For each shape calculate: **i** the perimeter   **ii** the area.

a
12 cm
9 cm
18 cm
7 cm

b
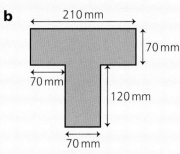
210 mm
70 mm
70 mm
120 mm
70 mm

c
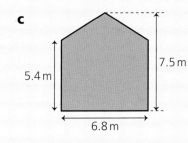
7.5 m
5.4 m
6.8 m

2 a The diameter of a circular pond is 6 metres.

Calculate: **i** the circumference of the pond   **ii** the area of the pond.

b The circumference of a circular plate is 30 centimetres.

Calculate: **i** the radius of the plate   **ii** the area of the plate.

3 Calculate the volume of each prism.

a
20 mm
36 mm
50 mm

b
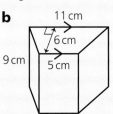
11 cm
6 cm
9 cm
5 cm

c
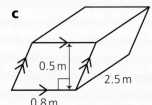
0.5 m
2.5 m
0.8 m

d
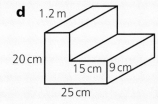
1.2 m
20 cm
15 cm 9 cm
25 cm

4 The diagram shows a square tile with sides of length 20 cm.

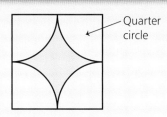

Quarter circle

   a Calculate the area of the shaded part.

   b A rectangular wall is 3.2 metres long and 2.4 metres high.

   Find the number of these tiles that is needed to cover the wall.

5 The diagram shows the dimensions of an oil drum.

The drum is a closed cylinder.

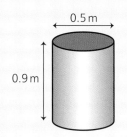

0.5 m

0.9 m

   a Sketch a net of the drum.

   b Calculate the total surface area of the drum.

   Give your answer to 2 decimal places.

   c Calculate the capacity of the drum.

   Give your answer in litres.

6 The diagram shows a wooden door.

ABCD is a rectangle and *CED* is a semicircle.

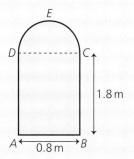

   a Calculate the area of the door.

   Give your answer in: **i** square metres   **ii** square centimetres.

   b The door is 4 centimetres thick.

   Calculate, in cubic centimetres, the volume of the door.

   c The mass of 1 cubic centimetre of wood is 0.6 gram.

   Calculate the mass of the door. Give your answer in kilograms.

7 What fraction of each shape is shaded green?

a
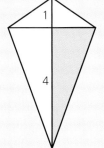

Kite with diagonal divided in the ratio 1 : 4

b
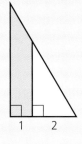

Triangle with base divided in the ratio 1 : 2

c
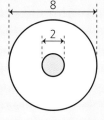

8

2

Circles with diameters 2 units and 8 units

d
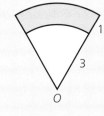

1

3

O

Sectors, centre *O*, with radii 3 units and 4 units

8 A rectangle is 2 m long and 80 cm wide.

Calculate the area in:

   a cm^2 **b** m^2

9 The diagrams show the nets of 3 solids.

The given dimensions are all in centimetres.

a 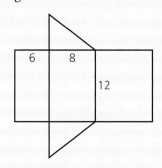   **b** 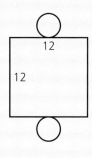   **c**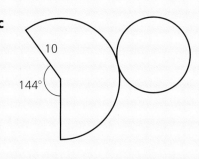

In each case: **i** name the solid

            ii calculate the surface area of the solid

            iii calculate the volume of the solid.

10 Find:

   a the perimeter

   b the area

of the shaded shape.

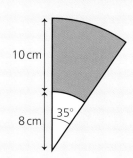

11 A cone has a volume of $96\pi\,\text{cm}^3$ and a radius of $6\,\text{cm}$.

Calculate:

   a the perpendicular height of the cone

   b the total surface area of the cone, leaving your answer in terms of π.

The volume of a cone is given by $V = \frac{1}{3}\pi r^2 h$.

The area of the curved surface is $A = \pi r l$.

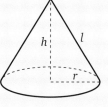

12 A closed cylindrical container has a height of $1.2\,\text{m}$ and a radius of $60\,\text{cm}$.

Calculate:

   a the total surface area, giving your answer in:

     i m^2

     ii cm^2

   b the volume, giving your answer in:

     i m^3

     ii cm^3

13 The diagram shows a swimming pool
of length 34 m and width 25 m.

The cross-section of the pool, *ABCD*, is
a trapezium. *AD* = 1.2 m and *BC* = 3.8 m.

a Calculate:

  i the area of the trapezium *ABCD*

  ii the number of litres of water in the pool when it is full.

b *AB* = 34.1 m

The interior surface of the pool is painted. It costs $2.50 to paint one square metre.

Calculate the cost of painting the pool, correct to the nearest hundred dollars.

c When the pool is emptied, the water flows through a cylindrical pipe of radius 10 cm.

The water flows along the pipe at a rate of 20 centimetres per second.

Calculate the time taken to empty the pool completely from full, giving your answer to the
nearest hour.

14 a The volume of a sphere of radius r is $\frac{4}{3}\pi r^3$.

A solid metal sphere has a radius of 2.5 cm.

One cubic centimetre of the metal has a mass of 4.8 grams.

Calculate the mass of the sphere.

b

Diagram A

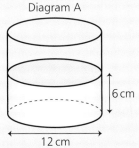

Diagram B

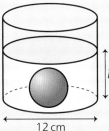

Diagram A shows a cylinder with a diameter of 12 cm.

It contains water to a depth of 6 cm.

The sphere described in part **a** is placed in the water, as shown in diagram B.

Calculate h, the new depth of water in the cylinder.

c A different sphere has a mass of 0.5 kg. It is made from the metal described in part **a**.

Calculate the radius of this sphere.

Learning outcomes

After this chapter you should be able to:

- understand and use directed numbers
- add, subtract, multiply and divide positive and negative integers
- use positive and negative numbers
- read clocks, dials and timetables
- calculate times using the 12-hour and 24-hour clock
- calculate with money and convert currencies
- calculate a given percentage of a quantity and express one quantity as a percentage of another
- calculate percentage increase or decrease
- calculate using reverse percentages
- solve problems on personal and household finance involving earnings, simple and compound interest, discount, profit and loss.

Revise 5.1 Directed numbers

A **directed number** has a positive or negative sign.

A negative sign ($-$) shows that the number is less than zero.

A positive sign ($+$) shows that the number is greater than zero.

When writing positive integers, the $+$ signs can be missed out.

An **integer** is any positive or negative whole number or zero.

All rational numbers, whether positive, negative or zero, can be shown on a number line.

When working with directed numbers, you can use horizontal or vertical number lines to help you.

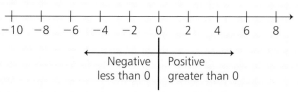

Adding and subtracting positive and negative numbers

There are two uses for $+$ and $-$ signs:

- to show if a number is positive or negative: $+4$ or -4
- to show if you are adding or subtracting: $6 + 4$ or $6 - 4$

You may see both uses of the signs together: $4 - -3$ or $4 - (-3)$

You will then have two signs next to each other.

Use the following rules:

Adding a positive number	+ +	is the same as	+	adding
Adding a negative number	+ −	is the same as	−	subtracting
Subtracting a positive number	− +	is the same as	−	subtracting
Subtracting a negative number	− −	is the same as	+	adding

You will also need to know how to enter calculations on your calculator.

Multiplying and dividing positive and negative numbers

You will need to know the following rules.

For multiplication:

$(+) \times (+) = (+)$

$(+) \times (-) = (-)$

$(-) \times (+) = (-)$

$(-) \times (-) = (+)$

For division:

$(+) \div (+) = (+)$

$(+) \div (-) = (-)$

$(-) \div (+) = (-)$

$(-) \div (-) = (+)$

Another way of remembering this is:

signs the same, positive answer

signs different, negative answer.

Worked examples

Temperature calculations

The table shows the maximum and minimum temperatures of some planets in our Solar System.

Using your knowledge of positive and negative integers, copy and complete the table.

Planet	Minimum temperature (°C)	Maximum temperature (°C)	Difference in temperatures (°C)
Earth	−89	71	
Mercury	−184	465	
Mars	−140	20	

Solution

Earth: Difference = $71 - -89 = 71 + 89 = 160\,°C$

Mercury: Difference = $465 - -184 = 465 + 184 = 649\,°C$

Mars: Difference = $20 - -140 = 20 + 140 = 160\,°C$

Directed number calculations

Work out:

a $-3 - (-4)^2$

b $-2(3 - 4)$

c $\dfrac{-2 - 4 \times -1}{2}$

d $3 + \left(\frac{1}{2}\right)^2 \times -\frac{1}{3}$

Solution

a $-3 - (-4)^2 = -3 - 16 = -19$

b $-2(3 - 4) = -2 \times (-1) = 2$

c $\dfrac{-2 - 4 \times -1}{2} = \dfrac{-2 + 4}{2} = \dfrac{2}{2} = 1$

d $3 + \left(\dfrac{1}{2}\right)^2 \times -\dfrac{1}{3} = 3 + \dfrac{1}{4} \times -\dfrac{1}{3} = 3 - \dfrac{1}{12} = 2\dfrac{11}{12}$

> **Exam tip**
>
> When squaring negative numbers with a calculator, always put the negative number in brackets,
>
> e.g.

Revise 5.2 Time and money

Digital and analogue displays

Some displays are **digital**. They show readings as numbers.

For example, the **odometer** in a car shows how far it has travelled:

0	1	7	4	3	2

The reading shown is 17 432 km.

Scales for weighing can be digital or **analogue**.

Analogue scales have a moving hand to show the weight.

These scales both show a reading of 3.7 kg.

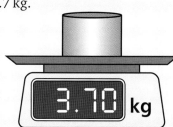

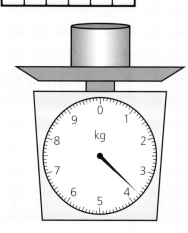

12-hour and 24-hour clocks

Time can use the 12-hour or the 24-hour clock.

The 12-hour clock times use 'am' to indicate morning and 'pm' to show an afternoon time.

24-hour clock times use times 13, 14, 15, … to represent pm times. In the 24-hour clock, hours and minutes are not separated by a point, and all times are written using four digits.

To change pm times to the 24-hour clock, add 12 to the hours.

10.20pm is 22 20.

But 3.45am is written as 03 45, as the hours before noon are the same in both systems.

Timetables are usually written using the 24-hour clock.

Calculating with time

To calculate the interval between two times:

1 Calculate the number of minutes to the next hour (o'clock).

2 Then calculate the number of complete hours.

3 Then work out the number of minutes remaining.

The first worked example shows how to do this.

Calculating with money

Bills

A bill usually gives the unit price of an item.

You must multiply the quantity by the unit price before finding the total bill.

Currency conversion

To **convert** from one currency to another you use a conversion rate.

A conversion rate tells you how much of one currency you receive for 1 unit of the other.

> **Exam tip**
>
> Do not round off your calculation until the final answer.

Worked examples

Journey calculation

Corbie needs to travel from Paris to Berlin.

He looks at the train timetable.

Destination							
Paris	06 41	07 44	08 41	09 49	12 41	13 49	16 41
Köln	10 26		12 26		16 26		20 26
Frankfurt		11 53		13 58		17 58	
Berlin	14 51	16 03	16 51	18 08	20 51	22 08	00 51+

All trains from Paris to Berlin go via Köln or Frankfurt.

The journey times from Paris to Köln are all the same.

So are the journey times from Paris to Frankfurt, Köln to Berlin and Frankfurt to Berlin.

a Corbie needs to be in Berlin by 4.30pm.

Which train should he catch?

b Calculate how long the journey takes.

c Is the journey quicker via Köln or via Frankfurt, and by how much?

d Corbie catches a train back to Paris, via Köln, leaving Berlin at 22 46.

If the journey times are the same as the outward journey, at what time will the train reach:

i Köln

ii Paris?

Solution

a 4.30pm is 16 30.

He must catch the 07 44, arriving at 16 03.

b The 07 44 arrives at 16 03.

From 07 44 to 08 00 = 16 minutes

From 08 00 to 16 00 = 8 hours

From 16 00 to 16 03 = 3 minutes

Total time = 8 hours 19 minutes

c The journey via Frankfurt = 8 h 19 min

The journey via Köln: The 06 41 arrives at 14 51.

From 06 41 to 07 00 = 19 minutes

From 07 00 to 14 00 = 7 hours

From 14 00 to 14 51 = 51 minutes

Total time = 7 hours 70 minutes

= 8 hours 10 minutes ← As 70 minutes = 1 hour 10 minutes.

The journey via Köln is 9 minutes quicker.

d The journey time from Köln to Berlin:

10 26 to 14 51:

10 26 to 11 00 = 34 minutes

11 00 to 14 00 = 3 hours

14 00 to 14 51 = 51 minutes

Total time = 3 hours 95 minutes

= 4 hours 35 minutes ← As 95 minutes = 1 hour 35 minutes.

i So, a train leaving Berlin at 22 46 arrives at Köln at:

22 h 46 min

+ 4 h 35 min

26 h 81 min

= 27 h 21 min ← As 81 minutes = 1 hour 21 minutes.

= 03 21 the following day ← As there are 24 hours in a day.

ii The journey time from Paris to Berlin via Köln is 8 hours 10 minutes.

So the 22 46 from Berlin will reach Paris at

22 h 46 min

+ 08 h 10 min

30 h 56 min

= 06 56 the next day ← As there are 24 hours in a day.

Working out a bill

Complete this decorator's bill:

Materials			
1.5 kg of filler	at $0.98 per kg	= $	
4 litres of undercoat	at $2.20 per litre	= $	
6.5 litres topcoat	at $2.56 per litre	= $	
3 litres white emulsion	at $1.75 per litre	= $	
1.5 litres wood stain	at $2.60 per litre	= $	

Labour

To prepare walls and ceiling:

To apply 1 coat of undercoat, 2 coats of topcoat

2 coats emulsion to ceiling

2 coats of wood stain to woodwork:

8.5 hours	at $15 per hour	= $	
TOTAL		= $	

Solution

Materials			
1.5 kg of filler	at $0.98 per kg	= $1.47	
4 litres of undercoat	at $2.20 per litre	= $8.80	
6.5 litres topcoat	at $2.56 per litre	= $16.64	
3 litres white emulsion	at $1.75 per litre	= $5.25	
1.5 litres wood stain	at $2.60 per litre	= $3.90	

Multiply number of units (kg, litres, hours) by the unit cost.

Labour

To prepare walls and ceiling:

To apply 1 coat of undercoat, 2 coats of topcoat

2 coats emulsion to ceiling

2 coats of wood stain to woodwork:

8.5 hours	at $15 per hour	= $127.50	
TOTAL		= **$163.56**	

Currency conversion

One Singapore dollar is worth 4.26 Danish kroner.

a Change 350 Singapore dollars into Danish kroner.

b Change 1000 Danish kroner into Singapore dollars.

c An item costs 36 dollars in Singapore and 150 kroner in Denmark.

In which country is it cheaper?

Solution

a 1 dollar = 4.26 kroner

350 dollars = 350 × 4.26 = 1491 kroner

c You can change 36 dollars into kroner or 150 kroner into dollars.

36 dollars = 36 × 4.26 = 153.36 kroner

The item is cheaper in Denmark.

b 4.26 kroner = 1 dollar

$1 \text{ krone} = \dfrac{1}{4.26} \text{ dollar}$

$1000 \text{ kroner} = 1000 \times \dfrac{1}{4.26} = 234.74 \text{ dollars}$

Revise 5.3 Percentages

Percentages of a quantity

To find a percentage of a quantity you can change the percentage to a fraction or a decimal:

A fraction:

42% of $19

$= \dfrac{42}{100} \times \$19$

$= \$7.98$

A decimal:

42% of $19

$= 0.42 \times \$19$

$= \$7.98$

You should be able to work these out on a calculator.

> **Exam tip**
>
> Make sure you know how to input fractions into your calculator using the fraction key.

Write one quantity as a percentage of another

To write one quantity as a percentage of another:

- first, write it as a fraction
- then multiply by 100 to get a percentage.

Percentage increase and decrease

When a quantity goes up, it is called an **increase**.

When a quantity goes down, it is called a **decrease**.

When the value of an item increases, it **appreciates**.

When the value of an item decreases, it **depreciates**.

Percentage increases or decreases are calculated as percentages of the original amount.

So the original value is always 100%.

Calculating the new amount

If an article increases in value, add the percentage to 100%.

For example, if an antique appreciates by 12%, its value increases from 100% to (100% + 12%) = 112%.

If an article decreases in value, subtract the percentage from 100%.

For example, if a bicycle depreciates by 24%, its value decreases from 100% to (100% − 24%) = 76%.

Calculating the percentage

If you are given the original value and the new value, calculate the change (the difference between the two values).

$$\text{Percentage change} = \frac{\text{change}}{\text{original amount}} \times 100$$

Finding 100% when another percentage is given

David gives £45 to charity. This is 6% of his savings.

His total savings are $\frac{£45}{6} \times 100 = £750$ ← $1\% = \frac{£45}{6}$

$$100\% = \frac{\text{amount}}{\text{percentage}} \times 100$$

Reverse percentages

You use reverse percentages to calculate the original amount.

For example, a coat is reduced by 40% in a sale. The sale price is $51.

This represents (100% − 40%) = 60% of the original price.

So the original price × 0.6 = $51. ← 60% = 0.6 as a decimal.

Original price = $51 ÷ 0.6 = $85.

Worked examples

Age ranges of a group of people as percentages

An airline records the ages of people on a plane.

a What percentage of the passengers are over 30 years old?

b The airline wants to encourage more young people to fly with them.

   i How many passengers were aged 30 or under?

   ii Out of those aged 30 or under, what percentage were more than 20 years old?

Age (years)	Frequency
$0 < x \leqslant 10$	1
$10 < x \leqslant 20$	4
$20 < x \leqslant 30$	29
$30 < x \leqslant 40$	54
$40 < x \leqslant 50$	27
$50 < x \leqslant 60$	11
$60 < x \leqslant 70$	5

Solution

a There are $1 + 4 + 29 + 54 + 27 + 11 + 5 = 131$ passengers.

$54 + 27 + 11 + 5 = 97$ passengers are over 30 years old.

$\frac{97}{131} \times 100 = 74.0458\ldots$

$= 74.0\%$ (to 1 d.p.)

b **i** $1 + 4 + 29 = 34$ are aged 30 or under.

ii $\frac{29}{34} \times 100 = 85.2941\ldots$

$= 85.3\%$ (to 1 d.p.) were at least 20 years old.

> **Exam tip**
>
> If necessary, round answers to 1 decimal place.

A new amount from a percentage decrease

Tak buys a car for £4200.

During the next three years, it decreases in value every year by 12% of its value at the start of that year.

Find the value of the car after three years.

Solution

The decrease is 12%, so the new value is 88%. ◄ $100\% - 12\% = 88\%$

Each year, the final value is 0.88 of the starting value.

After three years, the value $= £4200 \times 0.88 \times 0.88 \times 0.88$

$= £4200 \times 0.88^3 = £2862.18$

Percentage increase

The population of a village increased from 2056 to 2345.

Calculate the percentage increase.

Solution

The increase is $2345 - 2056 = 289$

The percentage increase is $\frac{289}{2056} \times 100 = 14.0564\ldots$

$= 14.1\%$ (to 1 d.p.)

> **Exam tip**
>
> - Remember to divide by the original amount or number.
> - Percentage changes are always given as a percentage of the original value.

A new amount from a percentage increase

Raul gets a pay rise of 7%.

After the pay rise he receives £37 022 per year.

What did he earn before the pay rise?

Solution

His pay rise of 7% means he receives $(100\% + 7\%) = 107\%$ of his previous salary.

Original salary $\times 1.07 = £37\,022$. ◄ $107\% = 1.07$ as a decimal

Original salary $= \dfrac{£37\,022}{1.07} = £34\,600$.

Revise 5.4 Personal finance

Earnings

Wages

Some people are paid a **weekly wage**.

They have an **hourly rate of pay**, and a number of hours a week they have to work.

They can work **overtime**, which is usually paid at a higher rate.

It might be paid at **time-and-a-half** ($1\frac{1}{2}$ times the normal hourly rate).

Or it might be paid at **double time** (twice the normal hourly rate).

Salaries

Some people are paid an **annual salary**.

They get a fixed amount of money for a year's work.

The money is paid monthly, so the annual salary is divided by 12 and that amount is paid every month.

People on salaries are not usually paid overtime.

They sometimes get a **bonus** at the end of the year.

Taxes

People pay taxes so that the government can pay for public services.

The taxes depend on which country you live in.

Income tax is tax paid on money you earn.

Buying and selling

Profit and loss

If you sell something for more than you paid for it, you make a **profit**.

If you sell it for less than you paid for it, you make a **loss**.

Discount

A discount is an amount of money taken off the price of goods.
It is often written as a percentage.

VAT

Many countries charge Value Added Tax (VAT), sales tax or consumption tax on goods.

The level of this tax varies, but is usually around 15%.

Hire purchase

Sometimes you buy goods on hire purchase. This is a useful way of buying items and paying for them over a number of months. You pay some money to start with, called a **deposit**, followed by a number of monthly **instalments**. Buying by hire purchase usually costs more than paying all at once.

Interest

Simple interest

When you invest money in a bank, they usually pay you **interest**.

The formula for simple interest is:

$$I = \frac{PRT}{100}$$

where P is the **principal** (the amount you invest), R is the **rate** of interest (the percentage of the principal paid each year) and T is the time in years that you invest the money.

The interest is calculated on the same principal every year.

Compound interest

Most banks pay **compound interest**.

With compound interest, the first year's interest is added to the principal.

So the second year's interest is calculated on a larger principal.

It continues in this way every year.

You also pay compound interest on loans, including credit cards.

The final amount, F, is given by the formula:

$$F = P\left(1 + \frac{R}{100}\right)^T$$

where P is the principal invested, R is the rate of interest and T is the time in years.

Worked examples

Income tax calculation

Benny earns £15 835 per year.

He earns £12 000 tax free, and pays income tax at 24% on the remainder.

How much tax does he pay per year?

Solution

His taxable income = income − tax-free income

Taxable income = £15 835 − £12 000 = £3835

Income tax = 24% of taxable income

$\qquad$ = 24% of £3835

$\qquad$ = 0.24 × £3835

$\qquad$ = £920.40

Profit and VAT calculation

a Mustapha buys a car for $4000 and sells it for $4200.

Calculate his percentage profit.

b The price of $4200 included 20% VAT.

Calculate the amount of VAT.

Solution

a Mustapha's profit is $200.

His percentage profit $= \frac{200}{4000} \times 100 = 5\%$

b Price including VAT $= 100\% + 20\% = 120\%$

Original price $\times 1.20 = \$4200$

Original price $= \$4200 \div 1.20$

$= \$3500$

So the VAT $= \$4200 - \$3500 = \$700$

Compound interest

Tak has $5000 to invest.

She invests it for 3 years at 2.1% compound interest.

What is the value of the investment at the end of 3 years?

> **Exam tip**
>
> Make sure you read the question carefully, as simple interest and compound interest are calculated differently.

Solution

$P = \$5000$, $T = 5$ and $R = 2.1$

$F = P\left(1 + \dfrac{R}{100}\right)^{T}$

$F = 5000\left(1 + \dfrac{2.1}{100}\right)^{3}$

$F = \$5321.66$ (to 2 d.p.)

The investment is worth $5321.66

Practise 5.1 – 5.4

1 The table shows the mean monthly temperatures for two different places in Canada.

	Jan	Feb	Mar	April	May	June	July	Aug	Sept	Oct	Nov	Dec
Alert	−30 °C	−31 °C	−30 °C	−22 °C	−8 °C	2 °C	5 °C	3 °C	−6 °C	−15 °C	−23 °C	−29 °C
Niagara Falls	−9 °C	−8 °C	−1 °C	2 °C	12 °C	15 °C	21 °C	19 °C	11 °C	10 °C	2 °C	−4 °C

a Write down the maximum and minimum monthly temperatures for
  i Alert and **ii** Niagara Falls.

b What are the differences in temperatures between the two places in **i** February and **ii** May?

c In which month are the temperature differences **i** the greatest **ii** the least?

2 Work out the following:

a $+8 - (-6) + (-9)$ **c** $8 - 2 \times 3 + (-10)$

b $-24 \div 9\,(-8)$ **d** $6 \times (-3) - (-2) \times (-4)$

3 a 1 Bahraini dinar is worth 2.59 Australian dollars.

Find the value of 225 Bahraini dinars in Australian dollars.

b 1 Indian rupee is worth 7.66 Armenian dram.

Find the value of 2000 Armenian drams in Indian rupees.

4 Maiya buys a CD.

There are 16 tracks on the CD.

The length of each track is given below.

2 min 35 s	3 min 12 s	4 min 7 s	2 min 11 s	2 min 51 s	3 min 12 s
3 min 17 s	2 min 34 s	3 min 19 s	4 min 1 s	4 min 5 s	2 min 11 s
3 min 5 s	3 min 42 s	2 min 44 s	5 min 2 s		

The CD starts to play the first track immediately, but there is a 2-second pause between each track.

How long does it take to play the entire CD?

5 Which is greater, and by how much: 35% of $40 or 65% of $22?

6 Maria earns $67 500 per annum. She earns $34 000 tax free, and then pays income tax at 18% on the remainder.

Calculate how much tax she pays.

7 An aeroplane flies from city A to B, and then on to C.

The flight from A to B takes 2 hours 27 minutes.

The plane waits at B for 42 minutes before taking off.

The flight from B to C takes 3 hours 18 minutes.

Complete the timetable below for three such flights.

	Flight 1	Flight 2	Flight 3
Depart A	08 36		
Arrive B		13 25	
Depart B			
Arrive C			01 45

8 Griselda is using this recipe:

4 skinned, boned chicken breasts, about 125 g each

20 g butter, melted

15 g clear honey

15 ml lemon juice

15 ml balsamic vinegar

The cost of the ingredients is shown in the table:

Ingredient	Price	Unit
Chicken breasts	$17.50	1 kg
Butter	$1.45	250 g
Honey	$1.20	330 g
Lemon juice	$1.45	500 ml
Balsamic vinegar	$1.20	250 ml

Calculate the cost of the ingredients used in the recipe.

9 Millie bought a bag in this sale.

She paid $14.95

a What was the original price of the bag?

b The next day, all items were sold at half the original price.

How much more would Millie have saved if she had waited until the next day to buy the bag?

10 Find the values of:

a $\dfrac{-5 - 7 + 2}{2 - -3}$

c $\left(-\frac{1}{5}\right)^3 \times (4^2 + 3^2)$

b $\dfrac{(-3)^2 - (-2)^2}{4 \times (-3 - 2)}$

d $(3 \div -4 \times 2) \div ((-10 + 3) \div 2)$

11 **a** Marco scored 39 out of 60 in a test. Calculate his mark as a percentage.

b To pass the test, you needed to score at least 70%.

How many marks out of 60 did you need to pass?

12 Carlos is starting a business.

He borrows $6000 from a loan company.

The loan company charges 4% per year compound interest.

How much interest will Carlos have paid after 3 years?

13 a The population of a city is 45 240.

It is predicted that over the next ten years the population will increase by 35%.

Calculate the predicted population ten years from now.

b The population has increased by 30% over the last ten years.

What was the population 10 years ago?

14 I invest $800 in a bank which pays 4.1% per year compound interest.

I leave the money there for three years.

a How much do I have in the bank after three years?

b What rate of simple interest would give the same amount?

15 A store sells computers.

The store owner sells a computer for £442 at a profit of 30%.

a How much does the store pay for the computer originally?

b In a sale, the store reduces the price by 20%.

What is the store's percentage profit in the sale?

16 William and Jonathan share some money.

William receives £25.20 which is 35% of the money.

How much does Jonathan receive?

17 Mark invests £650.

In the first year, it gains 4% compound interest.

In the following year, the interest rate drops to 3.5%.

Find the value of Mark's investment after two years.

6 Statistics

Learning outcomes

After this chapter you should be able to:

- collect and tabulate data, and interpret information in tables and statistical diagrams
- construct and use bar charts and pictograms
- construct and use pie charts
- calculate the mean, median, mode and range for discrete data and from frequency tables
- calculate an estimate of the mean and identify the modal class for grouped and continuous data
- construct and use cumulative frequency diagrams
- estimate and interpret the median, quartiles and interquartile range
- construct and read histograms with unequal intervals.

Revise 6.1 Statistical diagrams

Collecting and interpreting data

Tally charts

A **tally chart** is a method of showing a set of data.

Tallies are recorded in blocks of 5, making it easy to find the total, or **frequency**, for each category.

Tally charts are also used for **grouping** data, as in this example.

Test score	Tally	Frequency
41–50	卌 ‖	7
51–60	卌 卌 ‖‖	14
61–70	卌 卌 卌 卌 ‖	21
71–80	卌 ‖‖	8
Total		49

> ### Exam tip
>
> Always add up the frequency column and check that the total is equal to the number of elements of data.

Two-way tables

A two-way table is used when you need to show two different pieces of information.

The test scores above could be sorted by gender:

Score	41–50	51–60	61–70	71–80	Total
Male	3	9	8	4	24
Female	4	5	13	3	25
Total	7	14	21	7	49

Bar charts and pictograms

Bar charts

A **bar chart** has parallel bars or columns of the same width, with a space between them.

Each bar shows the quantity of a different category of data.

Bar charts can be used for numeric (or **quantitative**) data or descriptive (or **qualitative**) data.

Exam tip

When interpreting bar charts, look carefully at the scale.

Pictograms

A **pictogram** is a way of displaying qualitative data.

The data is displayed by using pictures, and a key shows the quantity that each picture represents.

The data can be shown in a bar chart or a pictogram.

The table below shows the colours of cars in a car park.

Exam tip

Choose a picture that is easy to divide into smaller amounts. Always include a key to show what the picture represents.

Colour	Frequency
Red	22
Blue	13
Black	28
Silver	17

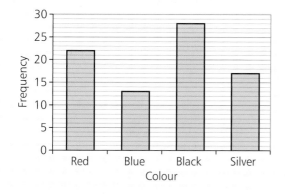

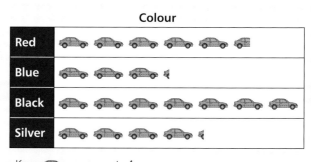

Key: represents 4 cars.

Pie charts

Pie charts

A **pie chart** is circular in shape. Pie charts show frequencies as proportions.

Pie charts are useful when representing a sample, where proportions are more important than the actual frequencies.

To construct a pie chart, the angle at the centre, 360°, must be divided into equal parts for each entry in the survey.

Mean, median, mode and range

An average is a single figure that represents a set of data.

You need to know three different averages: **mean**, **median** and **mode**.

You also need to be able to find the **range**. The range is not an average.

Mean

The mean is a way of calculating how much each value would be if they were shared out equally.

To find the mean, you add all the values together, and then share them out equally by dividing.

$$\text{Mean} = \frac{\text{sum of all the values}}{\text{total number of values}}$$

Median

The median is the middle value when the data is put in order.

The median can be a useful average because it has the same amount of data on either side of it.

The position of the median, m, is given by $\frac{n+1}{2}$, where n is the size of the data set.

If there is an even number of values in the data set, then there will be a middle pair of values.

The median is the mean of the middle pair.

> ### Exam tip
>
> Remember to order the data to find the median.

Mode

The mode is the most frequent value or number, or the value with the greatest **frequency**.

The mode can be called the **modal** number.

Range

The range tells you how spread out the data are.

Range = largest number − smallest number

The range is a single value.

Frequency tables

If the data are presented in a frequency table, take care that you interpret it correctly to find averages.

For example, the table shows the number of shots a golfer takes on each hole.

Number of shots	Frequency
1	0
2	2
3	3
4	5
5	7
6	1
Total	18

To find the *mean*, add up the number of shots from all 18 holes:

Number of shots	Frequency	The calculations in this column are very important	Number of shots × frequency
1	0	He scores a hole in 1 shot on 0 occasions. 0 × 1 =	0
2	2	He scores a hole in 2 shots on 2 occasions. 2 × 2 =	4
3	3	He scores a hole in 3 shots on 3 occasions. 3 × 3 =	9
4	5	He scores a hole in 4 shots on 5 occasions. 5 × 4 =	20
5	7	He scores a hole in 5 shots on 7 occasions. 7 × 5 =	35
6	1	He scores a hole in 6 shots on 1 occasion. 1 × 6 =	6
Total	18	Altogether he takes 74 shots	74

He takes 74 shots over 18 holes, so the *mean* is $\frac{74}{18} = 4.1$ (1 d.p.)

The median will be in the $\frac{18 + 1}{2} = 9.5$th position.

To find the 9th and 10th numbers think of the data as written out in order.

There are two 2s, three 3s, five 4s, seven 5s and one 6.

So the 2s are in positions 1 and 2, the 3s are in positions 3, 4, 5, the 4s are in positions 6, 7, 8, 9, 10.

So the 9th and 10th numbers are both 4.

The *median* is 4.

The *mode* is the number with the highest frequency, which is 5.

The range is 6 – 2 = 4, as his biggest score was 6 and the smallest was 2.

Worked examples

Pie charts

The table shows the colours of cars in a car park.

Colour	Frequency
Red	22
Blue	13
Black	28
Silver	17

Show these results in a pie chart.

Solution

Adding the frequencies shows that there are 80 cars.

So the red cars occupy $\frac{22}{80} \times 360° = 99°$

Colour	Frequency	Angle
red	22	$\frac{22}{80} \times 360° = 99°$
blue	13	$\frac{13}{80} \times 360° = 58.5°$
black	28	$\frac{28}{80} \times 360° = 126°$
silver	17	$\frac{17}{80} \times 360° = 76.5°$
Total	80	$360°$

Exam tip

Before drawing the pie chart, make sure the angles add up to 360°.

A pie chart showing the colours:

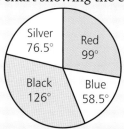

Calculating the mean, median, mode and range for a set of data

For this set of data,

    7   12   5   9   12   4   5   9   8   6   2   10   11   6   8   9   11   5   7   2

find:

a the mean   **b** the median   **c** the mode   **d** the range.

Solution

a Add up the numbers on your calculator. The sum is 149.

There are 20 numbers in this set of data, so divide the sum by 20:

mean $= 149 \div 20 = 7.45$

b To find the median put the numbers in order:

    2   2   4   5   5   5   6   6   7   ⑦   8   9   9   9   9   10   11   11   12   12

There are 20 numbers, so the middle one is in the $\dfrac{20 + 1}{2} = 10.5$th position.

The 10th number is 7 and the 11th number is 8 (circled).

The median is $\dfrac{7 + 8}{2} = 7.5$

c The mode is 9, as it occurs four times.

d The range is the difference between the largest number and the smallest number: $12 - 2 = 10$.

Exam tip

- When you add up the numbers, cross them out lightly as you work through them.
- Do the same when you put them in order to find the median.

Revise 6.2 Statistical measures

Continuous and discrete data

Grouping data

Discrete data can only take on certain values, for example, the number of people in a store.

Continuous data can take on any value, for example, the mass of a parcel.

The method of grouping is different for discrete data and continuous data.

Discrete data		Continuous data	
Number of people in a store each day in February	Frequency	Mass of a parcel, m (kg)	Frequency
1–5	5	$0 < m \leqslant 5$	3
6–10	9	$5 < m \leqslant 10$	6
11–15	8	$10 < m \leqslant 15$	9
16–20	6	$15 < m \leqslant 20$	5

The modal class

When data is put into groups, you cannot find the mode, because you do not have each individual piece of data.

Instead, you can find the most common group. This is called the **modal class**.

The modal class for the number of people in the store is 6–10, as this is the group with the highest frequency.

The modal class for the mass of a parcel is $10\,\text{kg} < m \leqslant 15\,\text{kg}$, as this is the group with the highest frequency.

Estimating the mean for grouped data

For grouped data, you cannot find the mean because you do not have each individual piece of data.

You must assume that all the data in a group is equal to the middle value for that group.

The middle value is calculated by finding the mean of the **class boundaries** (the greatest and least values in a class).

Cumulative frequency

Cumulative frequency tables

A cumulative frequency table records the quantity of data up to a given value.

Frequency table	
Height, h (cm)	Frequency
$130 \leqslant h < 140$	3
$140 \leqslant h < 150$	15
$150 \leqslant h < 160$	14
$160 \leqslant h < 170$	4

Cumulative frequency table	
Height, h (cm)	Cumulative frequency
$h < 130$	0
$h < 140$	3
$h < 150$	18
$h < 160$	32
$h < 170$	36

Cumulative frequency diagrams

The information in the cumulative frequency table can be plotted on a graph.

You can join the points with a curve or a series of straight lines.

The graph is called a cumulative frequency diagram.

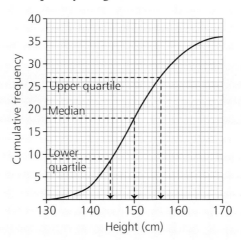

Medians, quartiles and range

The **median** is the halfway value in an ordered list of data.

The **lower quartile** is the value one quarter of the way from the lowest value.

The **upper quartile** is the value three quarters of the way from the lowest value.

In this example, there are 36 items. When finding an estimate of the median and quartiles from a cumulative frequency graph, or when a population is large, there is no need to add 1 to the number of items. So, the median is the value of the 18th item, as $\frac{1}{2}$ of 36 is 18. The median is 150 cm.

The lower quartile is the value of the 9th item, as $\frac{1}{4}$ of 36 = 9. The lower quartile is 144.5 cm.

The upper quartile is the value of the 27th item, as $\frac{3}{4}$ of 36 = 27. The upper quartile is 156 cm.

Cumulative frequency diagrams are useful for analysing the spread of data.

The **interquartile range** tells you the range of the middle half of the data, as it excludes the greatest and smallest quarters.

The interquartile range is the difference between the upper and lower quartiles.

So the interquartile range is 156 – 144.5 = 11.5 cm.

> **Exam tip**
>
> The interquartile range is a single value.

You can find the quartiles from discrete data.

For the set of 20 items of data:

2   2   4   5   5   5   6   6   7   7   8   9   9   9   9   10   11   11   12   12

the median is in position $\frac{20 + 1}{2}$ = 10.5, so is between the 10th and 11th. The median is 7.5.

There are 10 items on each side of the median.

So the quartiles are in positions $\frac{10 + 1}{2}$ = 5.5 from each end.

The lower quartile is 5, the upper quartile is 9.5 and the interquartile range is 9.5 − 5 = 4.5

Histograms

A **histogram** is used when data are grouped into classes with different widths.

A histogram represents the data in bars.

The frequency is indicated by the *area* of the bar.

The vertical axis shows the frequency density.

$$\text{Frequency density} = \frac{\text{frequency}}{\text{interval width}}$$

So the actual frequency can be calculated by multiplying the frequency density by the interval width.

Worked examples

Estimating the mean for grouped data

Calculate an estimate of the mean length of worms found in a garden.

Length of worm, l cm	Frequency
$0 < l \leq 5$	3
$5 < l \leq 10$	8
$10 < l \leq 15$	5
$15 < l \leq 20$	2

Solution

The table below shows the middle values for each group.

Length of worm, l cm	Frequency	Middle value	Middle value × frequency
$0 < l \leq 5$	3	2.5	7.5
$5 < l \leq 10$	8	7.5	60
$10 < l \leq 15$	5	12.5	62.5
$15 < l \leq 20$	2	17.5	35
Total	18		165

Estimate of mean $= \dfrac{165}{18} = 9.2$ (to 1 d.p.)

Histograms

The table gives information about the heights of 83 people.

Show this information in a histogram.

Height, h (cm)	Frequency, f
$130 < h \leq 150$	2
$150 < h \leq 170$	5
$170 < h \leq 180$	36
$180 < h \leq 185$	27
$185 < h \leq 190$	13

Solution

Add two columns to the table to show the class width, w, and the frequency density, $\dfrac{f}{w}$.

Height, h (cm)	Frequency, f	Class width, w	Frequency density, $\dfrac{f}{w}$
$130 < h \leq 150$	2	20	0.1
$150 < h \leq 170$	5	20	0.25
$170 < h \leq 180$	36	10	3.6
$180 < h \leq 185$	27	5	5.4
$185 < h \leq 190$	13	5	2.6

Then draw the histogram:

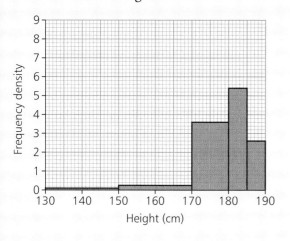

Exam tip

- Bar charts show frequency on the vertical axis. Histograms show frequency density on the vertical axis.

- The area of a bar on a histogram represents the frequency.

Practise 6.1 – 6.2

1 Manfred and Thomas have a long jump competition. They both jump four times.

Here are their distances, in metres.

	Jump 1 (m)	Jump 2 (m)	Jump 3 (m)	Jump 4 (m)
Manfred	4.12	3.98	3.88	4.06
Thomas	3.87	3.89	4.14	4.02

a Who had the larger mean distance, and by how much?

b Who had the larger range of distances, and by how much?

c Who had the larger median, and by how much?

d Who do you think did better overall? Give your reasons.

e The winner is the person with the longest jump. Who won?

2 a Six parcels have a mean weight of 4.5 kg. What is the total weight of the parcels?

b A seventh parcel weighs 5.2 kg. Calculate the mean weight of all seven parcels.

3 This pie chart shows the favourite type of film of students in a class:

a Which type was chosen by exactly $\frac{1}{4}$ of the class?

b The angle for romance films is 60°.
Four children chose romance as their favourite.

The angle for comedy films is 135°. How many chose comedy?

c How many children are there in the class?

Favourite type of film

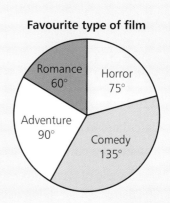

4 In a town there are 20 houses for sale.

The table below shows the number of bedrooms and the value of each house.

Number of bedrooms	2	4	1	3	2	3	4	1	3	2
Value of house, x ($1000s)	85	124	67	95	90	101	132	60	97	88

Number of bedrooms	4	3	2	3	4	1	3	4	3	2
Value of house, x ($1000s)	124	98	84	90	115	62	88	144	91	78

a **i** Use the information to complete the table:

   ii Use the table to draw a pie chart showing
        the number of bedrooms.

Number of bedrooms	Frequency
1	
2	
3	
4	

b Complete the table showing the value of the houses:

Value of house, x ($1000s)	Frequency
$60 \leqslant x < 80$	
$80 \leqslant x < 100$	
$100 \leqslant x < 120$	
$120 \leqslant x < 140$	
$140 \leqslant x < 160$	

5 Ravinder spins a five-sided spinner fifty times. The table shows the frequency of his scores:

Score	Frequency
1	11
2	7
3	11
4	
5	8

a Calculate the frequency for a score of 4.

b Calculate:

   i the mean score

   ii the median score

   iii the modal score

   iv the range of scores.

6 A store owner kept a record of how much customers spent on their shopping.

The results are shown in the table:

Amount spent, x (£)	$0 < x \leqslant 10$	$10 < x \leqslant 20$	$20 < x \leqslant 30$	$30 < x \leqslant 40$	$40 < x \leqslant 50$	$50 < x \leqslant 60$
Number of customers	25	28	12	9	5	1

a Write down the modal class interval.

b Calculate an estimate for the mean.

c Construct a cumulative frequency table to show the information.

d Use a scale of 2 cm to represent £10 on the horizontal axis and 2 cm to represent
     20 customers on the vertical axis to draw a cumulative frequency diagram.

e Use your cumulative frequency diagram to find estimates of:

  i the median amount of money spent

  ii the interquartile range

  iii the percentage of customers spending £35 or more.

7 The table shows the ages of the passengers on an aeroplane:

Age, x (years)	$0 < x \leqslant 10$	$10 < x \leqslant 20$	$20 < x \leqslant 40$	$40 < x \leqslant 70$	$70 < x \leqslant 80$
Number of passengers	6	29	56	48	11

The information is shown in the histogram:

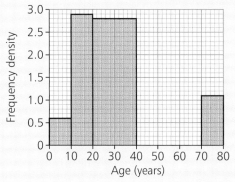

a The bar to represent the ages of $40 < x \leqslant 70$ is missing.

Calculate the frequency density for the missing bar.

b Calculate an estimate for the mean age of the passengers.

8 A store conducted a survey into how far shoppers travel to the store. They asked 200 shoppers.

The results are shown in the cumulative frequency diagram on the right.

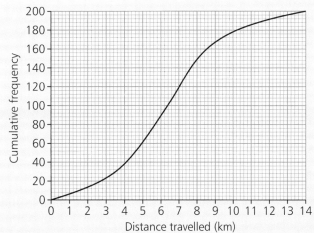

Use the diagram to find estimates for:

a the median distance travelled

b the upper quartile

c the percentage of those questioned who travelled 10 km or more.

d i Copy and complete this frequency table:

Distance travelled, d (km)	$0 < d \leqslant 2$	$2 < d \leqslant 5$	$5 < d \leqslant 7$	$7 < d \leqslant 8$	$8 < d \leqslant 10$	$10 < d \leqslant 14$
Frequency						

  ii Use the information in your table to draw a histogram. Use a scale of 1 cm to represent 1 km on the horizontal axis, and 1 cm to represent 5 on the vertical axis for frequency density.

Constructions and vectors

Learning outcomes

After this chapter you should be able to:

- measure lines and angles
- construct triangles and other simple geometrical figures from given data, using rulers, protractors, compasses and set squares
- construct angle bisectors and perpendicular bisectors, using straight edges and a pair of compasses only
- read and make scale drawings
- find sets of points which are:
  - at a given distance from a given point and from a straight line
  - equidistant from two points and from two straight lines
- use vector notation to describe a movement
- add and subtract vectors, and multiply a vector by a scalar
- calculate the magnitude of a vector
- use the sum and difference of two vectors to express given vectors in terms of two vectors, and use position vectors.

Revise 7.1 Constructions

Constructing triangles

Measuring and drawing angles

An **angle** is a measure of turn, or change in direction.

You measure angles with a protractor.

Protractors have two scales, one numbered clockwise and the other anticlockwise.

To measure an angle, place the cross at the centre of the protractor on the vertex of the angle.

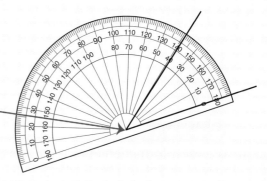

Place one of the zero lines of the protractor on one of the lines making the angle.

This angle is 39°.

Constructing an SAS triangle

The angle between two given sides is called the **included angle**.

An SAS triangle is probably the easiest type of triangle to construct.

For example, to draw a triangle *ABC* with *AB* = 6 cm,
AC = 5 cm, and angle *BAC* = 43° the steps are:

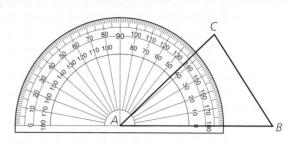

- draw the longer side (*AB*) 6 cm long

- then measure an angle of 43° at *A*

- extend this line and measure 5 cm to point *C*
  using compasses.

- then draw *BC* to complete the triangle.

Constructing an SSS triangle

Use a pair of compasses to construct a triangle when you are given the length of three sides.

For example, to draw a triangle with sides of 7 cm, 6 cm and 4 cm, the steps are:

- draw the longest side first (7 cm)

- open the compasses to 6 cm

- put the point on one end of the line and draw an arc

- open the compasses to 4 cm

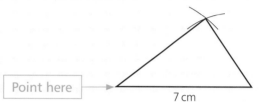

- put the point on the other end of the 7 cm line,
  and draw an arc to cross the first arc (as shown)

- finally, connect the two ends of the line to the intersection of the arcs.

Exam tip

Draw a sketch of the triangle and write the given measurements
on it. This will help you to see how to construct your triangle.

Constructing an SSA triangle

If the angle you are given is not the included angle, there can be two possible triangles.

If you are given the lengths of *AB* and *AC* and the size of angle *B*:

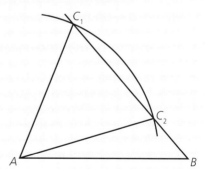

- draw *AB*, and measure the angle at *B*

- with compasses open to the length of *AC* and the point on *A*,
  draw an arc to cross the line from *B*

- the arc crosses at two points (labelled C_1 and C_2)

- then join either of these to *A* to give a triangle matching
  the description.

This is called the **ambiguous case**, which means there are two
triangles that match the description.

Constructing an ASA triangle

If you know two angles of a triangle, you can calculate the third angle,
as the sum of the angles is 180°.

For example, to construct a triangle ABC with $AB = 5$ cm, angle $BAC = 37°$ and angle $ACB = 100°$, the steps are:

- draw the line AB, 5 cm long

- measure an angle of 37° at A

- the angle at $B = 180° - 37° - 100° = 43°$, as the angles in a triangle add up to 180°

- draw angle $ABC = 43°$, making the lines longer if necessary so they intersect at C.

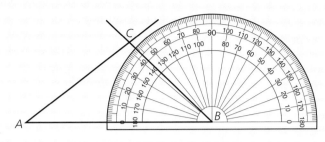

Constructing parallel lines

Use a ruler and set square to construct parallel lines.

Place a set square on a straight line.

Put a ruler against the **hypotenuse** (long side) of the set square.

Hold the ruler in position and slide the set square along the ruler.

You can draw a line parallel to the first line.

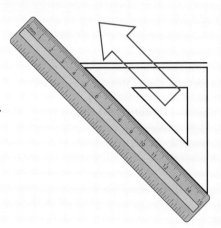

Bisectors and scale drawings

To **bisect** means to cut in half.

A **perpendicular bisector** cuts a line in half at right angles.

An **angle bisector** cuts an angle in half.

To construct a perpendicular bisector

The perpendicular bisector of a line AB joins all the points which are **equidistant** (the same distance) from A and B.

Open the compasses to more than half the length of AB.

Put the point on A and make two arcs, one on each side of the line.

Without changing the setting on your compasses, move the compass point to B and repeat. The arcs must cross the first two arcs.

Then draw a line passing through the two intersections.

This is the perpendicular bisector of AB.

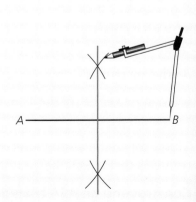

To construct an angle bisector

The bisector of angle *BAC* joins all the points equidistant from *AB* and *AC*.

To bisect (or cut exactly in half) an angle *BAC*, put the compass point on the vertex, *A*, and make equal marks at *B* and *C* along each arm of the angle.

Using *B* and *C* as centres, draw two arcs to cross inside the angle, at *D*.

Draw the angle bisector from *A* through *D*.

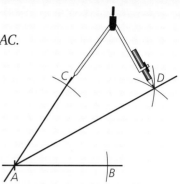

Scale drawings

A **scale drawing** is an accurate drawing that shows the exact shape but does not use the actual size.

The scale can be written in words, for example '1 cm represents 10 m'.   Remember 1 m = 100 cm

It can be written as a ratio, for example 1 : 1000.

Worked examples

Drawing accurately a quadrilateral from given information

Draw accurately a quadrilateral *ABCD* with *AB* = 8 cm, *BC* = 7 cm, *CD* = 9 cm, *AD* = 8 cm and angle *ABC* = 58°.

Solution

First draw a rough sketch:

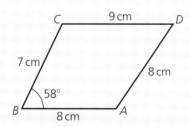

To make an accurate drawing:

- draw *BA*, 8 cm long

- measure an angle of 58° at *B* and draw *BC* = 7 cm

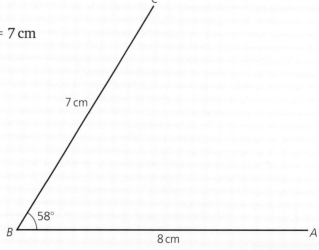

- then draw an 8 cm arc from *A* and a 9 cm arc from *C* to meet at *D*
- join *AC* and *CD*.

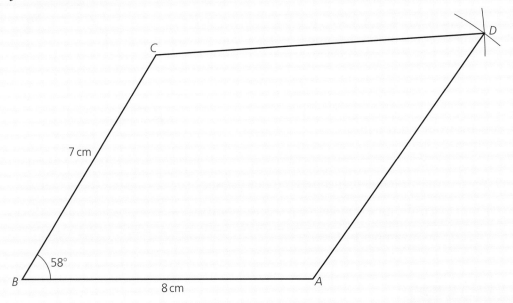

Constructing a scale drawing of a triangle

A triangular field *ABC* has sides of 100 m, 80 m and 75 m, as shown.

Use a scale of 1 cm to 10 m to make a scale drawing of the field.

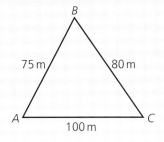

Solution

Draw *AC*, 10 cm long.

Open the compasses to 7.5 cm. Put the compass point on *A* and draw an arc.

Open the compasses to 8 cm. Put the compass point on *C* and draw an arc.

Label the point where the arcs cross as *B*.

Join *B* to *A* and *C*.

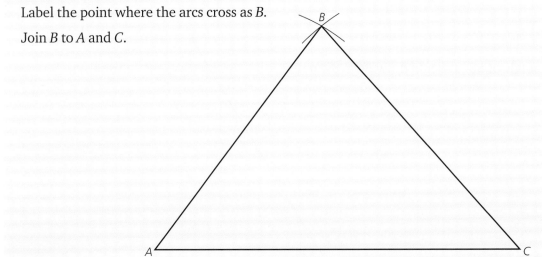

Worked examples

Constructions using points and lines

a Draw all the points equidistant from *AB* and *AC*.

b Draw all the points equidistant from *A* and *C*.

c Draw all the points 3 cm from *A*.

d Shade the region within the acute angle *CAB* where points are closer to *AC* than to *AB*, closer to *C* than *A* and less than 3 cm from *A*.

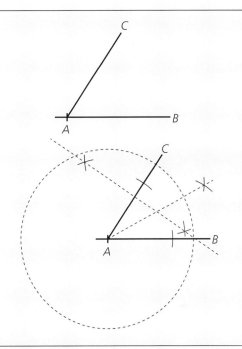

Solution

a This is the bisector of angle *BAC*.

b This is the perpendicular bisector of *AC*.

c This is a circle of radius 3 cm, centred on *A*.

d The required region is shaded in the diagram.

Scale drawing

A rectangular garden *ABCD* is 28 m long and 16 m wide.

A rectangular building *AEFG* is 8 m long and 6 m wide.

A goat is tied to the point *G* on a rope 12 m long.

a Mark the region of the garden that the goat can reach.

b The owner wants to plant a tree so that it is equidistant from *D* and *E* but beyond the reach of the goat.

Mark the region where the tree can be planted.

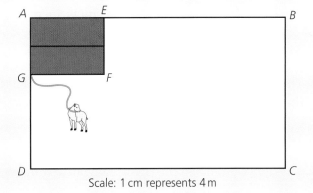

Scale: 1 cm represents 4 m

Solution

a The 12 m rope is represented by 3 cm.

Draw a quarter circle of radius 3 cm and centre *G*.

When the rope is pulled tight along *GF*, there is 4 m of rope beyond *F*. This is represented by 1 cm.

Draw a quarter circle of radius 1 cm, with the centre at *F*.

The dotted region in the diagram is the region that the goat can reach.

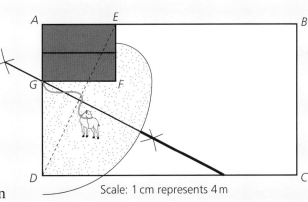

Scale: 1 cm represents 4 m

b For the tree to be equidistant from *D* and *E*, find the perpendicular bisector of *DE*.

The tree can be planted anywhere along the thick black line.

Exam tip

Leave your construction lines to show how you answered the question. Mark the answer region clearly.

Revise 7.2 Vectors

Combining vectors

Vector notation

A **vector** is a directed quantity. It has a defined length and it shows a particular direction.

Vectors are particularly useful because they can be combined to show the result of two movements.

A vector has a **magnitude** (or size) and a direction.

The movement from *A* to *B* can be written as $\overrightarrow{AB}$, or as **n**.

You cannot write in bold type, so you write **n** as n̲

As a column vector, it is $\begin{pmatrix} 3 \\ -2 \end{pmatrix}$.

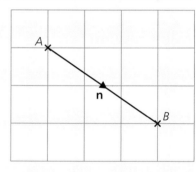

The top number represents a movement parallel to the *x*-axis and the bottom number represents a movement parallel to the *y*-axis.

The column vector $\begin{pmatrix} 3 \\ -2 \end{pmatrix}$ means:

> move 3 units to the right (a negative number would indicate left), and

> move 2 units down (because the number is negative it means a downward movement).

So 3 is the horizontal component and -2 is the vertical component.

The vector going in the opposite direction is $\overrightarrow{BA} = -\mathbf{n} = \begin{pmatrix} -3 \\ 2 \end{pmatrix}$.

Adding and subtracting vectors

You add vectors by adding the horizontal components and the vertical components separately.

In the diagram on the next page, $\overrightarrow{AB} = \begin{pmatrix} 5 \\ -2 \end{pmatrix}$ and $\overrightarrow{BC} = \begin{pmatrix} -3 \\ -4 \end{pmatrix}$.

$$\overrightarrow{AB} + \overrightarrow{BC} = \begin{pmatrix} 5 \\ -2 \end{pmatrix} + \begin{pmatrix} -3 \\ -4 \end{pmatrix}$$

$$= \begin{pmatrix} 2 \\ -6 \end{pmatrix} = \overrightarrow{AC}$$

The diagram shows that $\overrightarrow{AB} + \overrightarrow{BC} = \overrightarrow{AC}$. In vector terms, a movement from A to B and then to C is the same as a movement directly from A to C.

You subtract vectors by subtracting the horizontal components and the vertical components separately.

$$\overrightarrow{AC} - \overrightarrow{BC} = \begin{pmatrix} 2 \\ -6 \end{pmatrix} - \begin{pmatrix} -3 \\ -4 \end{pmatrix}$$

$$= \begin{pmatrix} 5 \\ -2 \end{pmatrix}$$

$$= \overrightarrow{AB}$$

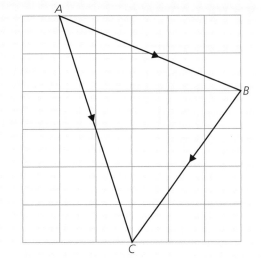

Exam tip

A minus sign in front of a vector reverses the direction of movement. So $-\overrightarrow{BC} = \overrightarrow{CB}$.

Multiplying a vector by a scalar

A vector has a size and a direction. A **scalar** quantity has a size but no direction.

You can multiply a vector by a scalar.

The vector $2\mathbf{a} = \mathbf{a} + \mathbf{a}$.

To multiply a vector by a scalar, multiply each component of the vector by the scalar:

$$4\begin{pmatrix} 2 \\ -3 \end{pmatrix} = \begin{pmatrix} 4 \times 2 \\ 4 \times -3 \end{pmatrix} = \begin{pmatrix} 8 \\ -12 \end{pmatrix}$$

The resultant vector is four times longer than the original vector, and goes in the same direction, so is parallel to the original vector.

If a vector is a multiple of another vector, then the two vectors are parallel.

Parallel vectors can go in opposite directions. $-3\mathbf{a}$ is three times the length of $\mathbf{a}$, running in the exact opposite direction.

The magnitude of a vector

The magnitude, or size, of a vector can be calculated using Pythagoras' theorem.

The vector $\begin{pmatrix} x \\ y \end{pmatrix}$ has a horizontal component of length x and a vertical component of length y.

The length of the vector is given by $l = \sqrt{x^2 + y^2}$.

The vector $\overrightarrow{AB} = \begin{pmatrix} 3 \\ -2 \end{pmatrix}$ has magnitude $\sqrt{3^2 + (-2)^2} = \sqrt{13}$ (or 3.6 to 1 d.p.).

The magnitude of a vector $\mathbf{a}$ is written $|\mathbf{a}|$.

So $|\mathbf{a}| = \sqrt{13}$ (or 3.6 to 1 d.p.).

Vector geometry

Position vectors

On a coordinate grid, the point (0, 0) is usually marked as O, and is called the **origin**.

A **position vector** gives the vector from the origin to a point.

The movement from the origin to the point $A(-1, 2)$ is $\overrightarrow{OA} = \begin{pmatrix} -1 \\ 2 \end{pmatrix}$

This is called the position vector of A.

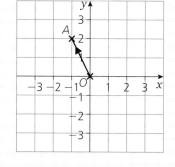

Collinear points

Collinear points lie on a straight line.

If A, B and C are collinear, then $\overrightarrow{AB}$ and $\overrightarrow{AC}$ will be parallel, so $\overrightarrow{AC}$ will be a multiple of $\overrightarrow{AB}$.

Worked example

Vector geometry

$OABC$ is a parallelogram.

The position vectors of A and C are **a** and **c**.

X lies on AC so that $AX = \frac{1}{3}AC$.

Y is the midpoint of AB.

Show that OXY is a straight line.

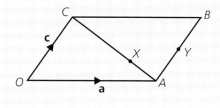

Solution

$\overrightarrow{OX} = \overrightarrow{OA} + \overrightarrow{AX}$ ← As you can move from O to X by moving along OA and then AX

$\quad = \overrightarrow{OA} + \frac{1}{3}\overrightarrow{AC}$ ← As $AX = \frac{1}{3}AC$

$\quad = \mathbf{a} + \frac{1}{3}(\mathbf{c} - \mathbf{a})$ ← As $\overrightarrow{OA} = \mathbf{a}$ and $\overrightarrow{AC} = \overrightarrow{AO} + \overrightarrow{OC} = -\overrightarrow{OA} + \overrightarrow{AC} = -\mathbf{a} + \mathbf{c}$

$\quad = \frac{2}{3}\mathbf{a} + \frac{1}{3}\mathbf{c}$

$\quad = \frac{1}{3}(2\mathbf{a} + \mathbf{c})$

$\overrightarrow{OY} = \overrightarrow{OA} + \overrightarrow{AY}$ ← As you can move from O to Y by moving along OA and then AY

$\quad = \overrightarrow{OA} + \frac{1}{2}\overrightarrow{AB}$ ← As $AY = \frac{1}{2}AB$

$\quad = \mathbf{a} + \frac{1}{2}\mathbf{c}$ ← As $\overrightarrow{OA} = \mathbf{a}$ and $\overrightarrow{AB} = \overrightarrow{OC} = \mathbf{c}$ as AB and OC are parallel and equal.

$\quad = \frac{1}{2}(2\mathbf{a} + \mathbf{c})$

$\overrightarrow{OX}$ and $\overrightarrow{OY}$ are both multiples of $(2\mathbf{a} + \mathbf{c})$, so are parallel.

But they both pass through O, so O, X and Y are collinear.

Practise 7.1 – 7.2

1 The diagram shows a sketch of a semicircle with a radius of 7 cm.
AB is a diameter and *O* is the centre.

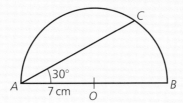

C is a point on the semicircle so that angle *BAC* = 30°.

a Make an accurate drawing of the semicircle and the line *AC*.

b **i** Construct the perpendicular bisector of *AC*.

   ii What do you notice about the line you have drawn?

2 *A*, *B* and *C* are three towns.

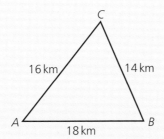

The distances between them are shown on the sketch map.

a Make an accurate drawing of the towns, using a scale of 1 cm to 2 km.

b A store, *S*, is on the line *AB*, equidistant from *A* and *B*.

Construct the perpendicular bisector of *AB* to find the position
of the store.

c Use your drawing to find the distance from *C* to the store.

3 **a** Construct a triangle *ABC* with *AB* = 11 cm, *AC* = 9 cm and *BC* = 7 cm.

b Construct the bisector of angle *ABC*. Label the point *D* where it crosses *AC*.

c Construct the perpendicular bisector of *CD*.

4

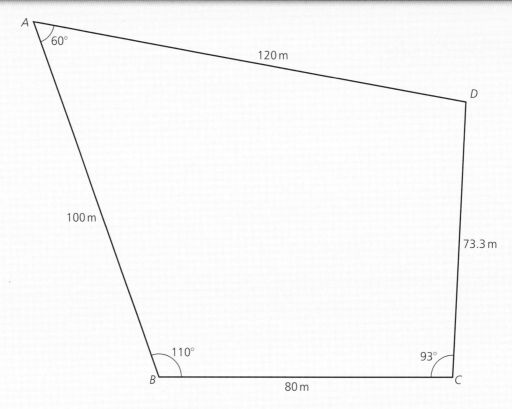

The diagram is a scale drawing of a field. The actual length of the side *AB* is 100 metres.

a Find the scale of the drawing in the form 1 : *n*, where *n* is an integer.

In part **b** use a straight edge and compasses only. Leave in your construction lines.

b **i** Make a copy of the scale drawing.

ii A tree in the field is equidistant from *A* and *D*.
Construct the line on which the tree stands.

iii The tree is also equidistant from the sides *BC* and *AB*.
Mark the position of the tree with the letter *T*.

5 The diagram shows a sketch of an island.

A and *B* are two radio masts, 120 km apart.

a Using a scale of 1 cm to 20 km, make a sketch
of the island, marking *A* and *B*, 120 km apart.

b The mast at *A* has a range of 60 km.

The mast at *B* has a range of 80 km.

Shade on your map the region of the island within
range of at least one mast.

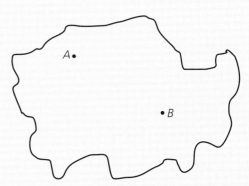

6 Four roads, *AB*, *BC*, *CD* and *AD* make a rhombus with sides of 220 m.

Angle *ABC* = 80°.

a Using a scale of 1 cm to represent 20 m, make an accurate scale drawing of the roads.

b A man wants to build a house in the land between the roads.

He must build the house so that:

i it is at least 30 m away from the roads

ii it is closer to *B* than *A*

iii it is closer to *AD* than *AB*.

Shade the region where the house can be built.

7 $\mathbf{a} = \begin{pmatrix} 3 \\ -1 \end{pmatrix}$ and $\mathbf{b} = \begin{pmatrix} -2 \\ 1 \end{pmatrix}$.

Work out:

a $\mathbf{a} + \mathbf{b}$ **b** $\mathbf{b} - \mathbf{a}$ **c** $2\mathbf{a} - \mathbf{b}$ **d** $|2\mathbf{a} - \mathbf{b}|$.

8 In the diagram, $\overrightarrow{DA} = \mathbf{a}$, $\overrightarrow{AB} = 3\mathbf{a} + 2\mathbf{b}$, $\overrightarrow{CB} = \mathbf{a} + \mathbf{b}$, and $\overrightarrow{DC} = 3\mathbf{a} + \mathbf{b}$.

a Find, in terms of **a** and **b**:

i $\overrightarrow{AC}$

ii $\overrightarrow{DB}$.

b Show that *ACBD* is a trapezium.

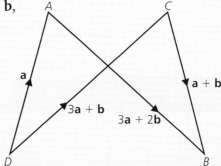

9 *OABC* is a parallelogram.

D is the point on *OC* such that $OD = \frac{1}{2}OC$.

E is the point on *OB* such that $OE = \frac{1}{2}OB$.

$\overrightarrow{OD} = \mathbf{a}$ $\overrightarrow{OA} = 2\mathbf{b}$

a Find, in terms of **a** and **b**:

i $\overrightarrow{OB}$ **ii** $\overrightarrow{OE}$

b Use a vector method to show that *OA* is parallel to and twice the length of *DE*.

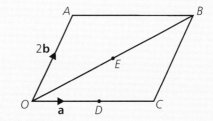

10 *OABCD* is a pentagon.

$\overrightarrow{OA} = \mathbf{a}$, $\overrightarrow{OB} = 2\mathbf{b}$, $\overrightarrow{OD} = \mathbf{b} - \mathbf{a}$ and $\overrightarrow{DC} = \mathbf{b}$

Prove that *OABC* is a parallelogram.

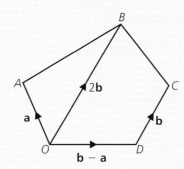

Learning outcomes

After this chapter you should be able to:

- use Cartesian coordinates to plot points on a graph
- draw and interpret real-life graphs
- find rates of change in distance–time and speed–time graphs
- draw a straight line graph from given data
- find the gradient and the equation of a given straight line
- find the equation of a line parallel to a given straight line
- find the coordinates of the midpoint of a line segment
- draw and interpret the graph of a quadratic function or a cubic function
- draw the graph of reciprocal functions
- estimate gradients of curves by drawing tangents
- solve equations approximately by graphical methods.

Revise 8.1 Real-life graphs

Plotting points

Cartesian coordinates use two **axes** at right angles.

The **x-axis** is drawn from left to right across the page.

The **y-axis** is drawn from top to bottom of the page.

A point on the grid is described by two coordinates.

The point where the axes cross is called the **origin**, which is the point (0, 0).

The **x-coordinate** measures the distance along the x-axis from the origin.

The **y-coordinate** measures the distance along the y-axis from the origin.

Conversion graphs

To draw a **conversion graph**, you need to know two equivalent measurements.

For example: a distance of 5 miles is equivalent to 8 kilometres.

We also know that 0 miles is the same as 0 kilometres.

These equivalent measurements are used in the
first worked example.

Distance–time graphs

This distance–time graph shows a two-hour bus journey.

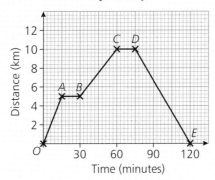

Time is always shown on the horizontal axis and distance on the vertical axis.

On this graph, the time is shown in minutes from the start of the journey.

The distance shown is the distance from the bus station.

So *OA* and *BC* show the bus moving away from the bus station and *DE* shows it returning.

Horizontal parts of the graph (*AB* and *CD*) show when the bus has stopped.

The bus travels for 15 minutes, (*OA*), stops for 15 minutes and then travels on for 30 minutes (*BC*).

It reaches its destination, 10 km from the start, after one hour.

The section *CD* shows that the bus stays at its destination for 15 minutes.

The section *DE* shows the return journey, which takes 45 minutes.

Speed–time graphs

On a speed–time graph, time is shown on the horizontal axis and speed is shown on the vertical axis.

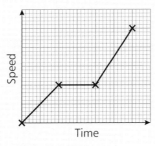

From a speed–time graph you can work out **acceleration**, using the formula:

$$\text{Acceleration} = \frac{\text{increase in speed}}{\text{time}}$$

If the speed is decreasing, use the formula:

$$\text{Deceleration} = \frac{\text{decrease in speed}}{\text{time}}$$

Exam tip

On a speed–time graph, the gradient (see page 95) tells you the acceleration. If part of the graph has a zero gradient, this shows that the bus has no acceleration, NOT that it has stopped moving.

Worked examples

Conversion graph

5 miles = 8 kilometres.

a Draw a graph to convert between miles and kilometres.

b Use your graph to change 3 miles to kilometres.

b Change 12 miles to kilometres.

Solution

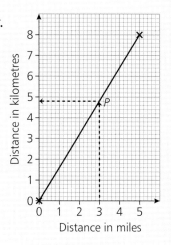

a Label axes from 0 to 5 miles horizontally and from 0 to 8 km vertically.

The points (0, 0) and (5, 8) lie on the graph so plot these and join them with a ruled line.

b Start at 3 miles. Draw a vertical line up to meet the graph (at *P*).

Draw a horizontal line across from P to the vertical axis and read off the value there.

   3 miles = 4.8 km

c 12 miles = 4 × 3 miles

        = 4 × 4.8 km

        = 19.2 km

> Label the axes to make it clear which shows miles and which shows kilometres.

Distance–time graph

Here is the distance–time graph for Paul's car journey from home to work.

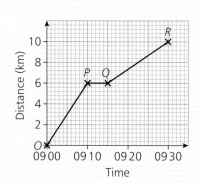

a What happens between 09 10 and 09 15?

b What is Paul's average speed from *Q* to *R*?

c How does the graph show that the average speed from *O* to *P* is greater than the average speed from *Q* to *R*?

Solution

a Between 09 10 and 09 15 Paul is not moving.

b Between *Q* and *R* the distance travelled is 4 km and the time is 15 minutes.

   4 km in 15 minutes = 16 km in 60 minutes

   The average speed is 16 km/h.

c The gradient is steeper from *O* to *P* than from *Q* to *R*.

Speed–time graph

This is the speed–time graph for a bus journey.

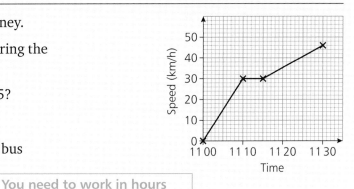

a Work out the acceleration of the bus during the first 10 minutes.

b What happens between 11 10 and 11 15?

Solution

a In the first 10 minutes, the speed of the bus goes from 0 to 30 km/h.

10 minutes is one-sixth of an hour.

> You need to work in hours because the speed is in km/h.

Acceleration $= 30 \div \frac{1}{6} = 180 \, \text{km/h}^2$

b The bus travels at a steady speed of 30 km/h.

Revise 8.2 Straight line graphs

Drawing a straight line graph

An equation such as $y = 4x + 5$ can be shown on a graph.

The graph will be a straight line and $y = 4x + 5$ is called a **linear equation**.

To draw the graph, work out the coordinates of three points on the line.

> Take $x = 0$ as one of the values because it is easy to substitute in the equation.

Exam tip

The third point is a check to make sure your working is correct.

If your three points are not in a straight line, go back and check your working.

Gradients of straight line graphs

The **gradient** is a measure of how steep the line is.

$$\text{Gradient} = \frac{\text{change in vertical distance}}{\text{change in horizontal distance}} = \frac{\text{change in } y}{\text{change in } x}$$

Exam tip

You can draw the triangles anywhere under the line. Make sure the horizontal distance is a whole number so it is easy to divide by.

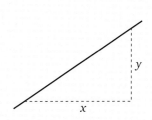

This line has a positive gradient.

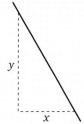

This line has a negative gradient.

A negative gradient indicates that as x increases, y decreases.

You can work out the gradient from the graph, using right-angled triangles as shown above.

You can also find the gradient from the equation of the line.

Write the equation in the form $y = mx + c$.

x and y are the **variables** in the equation (because they can take different values).

The number in front of x, 'm', is the **coefficient** of x and is the gradient of the line.

When $x = 0$, $y = c$, so this is where the line crosses the y-axis.

For example, the gradient of the line $y = -4x + 5$ is -4 and it crosses the y-axis at $(0, 5)$.

Finding the equation of a straight line graph

First find the gradient, m.

Then try to find c by looking to see where the line crosses the y-axis.

Or you can substitute a pair of coordinates to find c.

> **Exam tip**
>
> When you work out the gradient, read the scales carefully. Do *not* just count squares.

Parallel lines

Parallel lines have the same gradient.

Any line parallel to $y = 5x - 3$, will be $y = 5x + c$.

If the line goes through, for example, $(2, 3)$, substitute these values to find c.

$$3 = 5 \times 2 + c$$
$$3 = 10 + c$$
$$c = -7$$

so the line is $y = 5x - 7$.

Line segments

A **line segment** is the part of a line joining two points.

To find the midpoint of a line segment, find the mean of the coordinates of the end points.

Worked examples

A straight line graph

Draw the graph of $y = 7 - 2x$ for values of x from -1 to 5.

Solution

Choose three values of x and make a table of values.

Use the end values, -1 and 5, and 0 because it is easy to substitute.

x	-1	0	5
y	9	7	-3

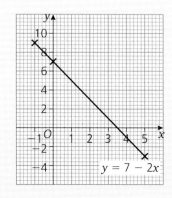

The gradient and equation of a given straight line

a Find the gradient of the line shown opposite.

b Find the equation of the line.

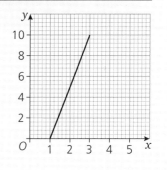

Solution

a The gradient of this line is $\dfrac{10-0}{3-1}=5$. ← Using the largest possible triangle.

b Its equation is $y = 5x + c$ and it goes through $(1, 0)$.

$0 = 5 + c$ ← Substitute the values $(1, 0)$ in the equation.

$c = -5$

The equation of the line is $y = 5x - 5$.

The equation of a line

A is the point $(-4, 2)$ and B is the point $(5, -1)$.

a Find the coordinates of the midpoint of the line segment AB.

b Find the equation of the line AB.

c Find the equation of a line parallel to AB, through the point $(1, 3)$.

Solution

Draw a sketch to show the positions of A and B.

a The midpoint is at $\left(\dfrac{-4+5}{2}, \dfrac{2+-1}{2}\right) = (0.5, 0.5)$.

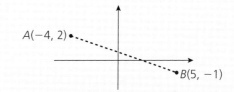

b The gradient of AB is $\dfrac{2--1}{-4-5} = \dfrac{3}{-9} = -\dfrac{1}{3}$. ← Note that as x increases y decreases, so the gradient is negative

The equation of AB is $y = -\dfrac{1}{3}x + c$.

When $x = -4, y = 2$, so substitute these numbers in the equation.

$2 = -\dfrac{-4}{3} + c$

$6 = 4 + 3c$ ← Multiply throughout by 3.

$c = \dfrac{2}{3}$

The equation of AB is $y = -\dfrac{1}{3}x + \dfrac{2}{3}$, which can also be written as $3y + x = 2$.

c Any parallel line will have a gradient of $-\dfrac{1}{3}$, so will be of the form $y = -\dfrac{1}{3}x + c$.

When $x = 1, y = 3$, so $3 = -\dfrac{1}{3} + c$

$c = 3\dfrac{1}{3}$

The parallel line had equation $y = -\dfrac{1}{3}x + 3\dfrac{1}{3}$.

Revise 8.3 Graphs of functions

All the graphs in this section are curves, so you have to plot more than three points in order to draw them. Your table of values should include all the integer values of x in the given range.

Quadratic functions

Every **quadratic function** contains a term in x^2 but no higher powers of x such as x^3 or x^4.

$f(x) = 3x^2 - 3x - 2$ is a quadratic function but $g(x) = 3x^2 + x^3$ is not.

To work out values of y for an expression such as $y = 3x^2 - 3x - 2$, put some extra lines into your table:

x	-2	-1	0	1	2	3	4
$3x^2$	12	3	0	3	12	27	48
$-3x$	$+6$	$+3$	0	-3	-6	-9	-12
y	16	4	-2	-2	4	16	34

Add the values in the middle two lines together and then subtract 2, to get the values of y.

Plot the points and join them with a smooth curve.

Quadratic functions with $(+)\,x^2$
have this shape:

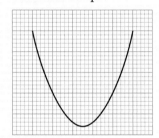

Quadratic functions with $-x^2$
have this shape:

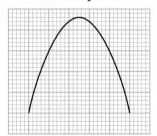

Exam tip

If you join your plotted points with straight lines, you will lose marks.

Cubic functions

$f(x) = x^3 + x - 2$ is an example of a **cubic function**.

Every cubic function contains a term in x^3 but no higher powers of x.

Cubic functions with $(+)x^3$
have this shape:

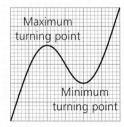

Cubic functions with $-x^3$
have this shape:

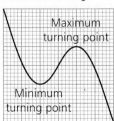

Some cubic functions have their two turning points together and look like one of these:

Graphs of reciprocal functions

The **reciprocal function** of x is $\frac{1}{x}$.

This is the graph of $y = \frac{1}{x}$.

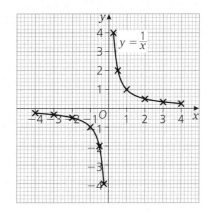

Exam tip

- Plot some points where x lies between 0 and 1 to help you to draw the right-hand part of the curve.
- Plot some points where x lies between -1 and 0 to help you to draw the left-hand part of the curve.

Here are the graphs of some more reciprocal functions:

$$y = \frac{-2}{x} \qquad\qquad y = \frac{50}{x} \qquad\qquad y = \frac{1}{x^2}$$

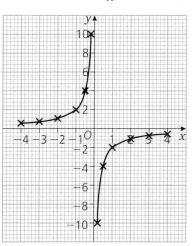 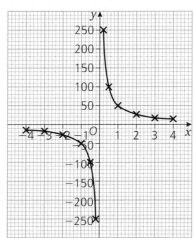 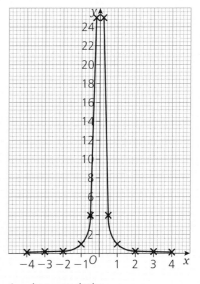

The negative sign turns the graph upside down. The 2 in the numerator stretches the graph with a factor of 2 parallel to the y-axis.

The 50 in the numerator stretches the graph with a factor of 50 parallel to the y-axis.

As x is squared, there are no negative values of y.

For reciprocal functions, when $x = 0$ the value of y cannot be found.

There is a break in the graph and it is said to be **discontinuous**.

Drawing a tangent to a curve

AB is a tangent to the curve at P.

Use a ruler to draw a tangent.

Your line must touch the curve but not cross it.

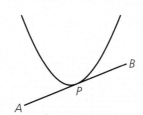

Estimating the gradient of a curve

The gradient of a curve is constantly changing.

The gradient of a curve at a point on the curve is equal to the gradient of the tangent to the curve at that point.

To find the gradient of a curve at a given point, draw the tangent at the point and find its gradient.

This is the graph of $y = x^2$.

The tangent to the graph at $x = -1$ has been drawn.

The gradient is $\dfrac{5 - 1}{-3 - -1} = -2$.

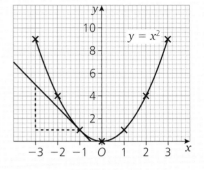

Solving equations by graphical methods

To solve the equation $f(x) = 0$, find where the graph of $y = f(x)$ crosses the line $y = 0$ (the x-axis).

To solve the equation $f(x) = g(x)$, draw $y = f(x)$ and $y = g(x)$ on the same grid.

The point where the two graphs meet is called the **intersection** of the graphs.

(There may be more than one intersection.)

The x-coordinate at the intersection is a solution of the equation $f(x) = g(x)$.

Given the graph of $y = x^3$, you can solve the equation $x^3 - 2x + 3 = 0$ by drawing an additional line on the graph.

First, rearrange the equation so that one side consists of x^3.

$$x^3 = 2x - 3.$$

The solutions can be found by drawing $y = 2x - 3$ on the graph of $y = x^3$

Reading solutions from a graph only gives an estimate for the solutions. In some cases the solutions could be irrational or involve more decimal places than can be read accurately.

Worked examples

Graph of a cubic function

a Copy and complete the table of values for $f(x) = 6x - x^3$.

b Draw the graph of $y = f(x)$ for values of x from -3 to 3.

c Write down an estimate of the coordinates of the maximum turning point on your graph.

d Use your graph to find estimates for the solutions of the equation $f(x) = 0$.

x	-3	-2	-1	0	1	2	3
$6x$	-18	-12					18
$-x^3$	$+27$	$+8$					-27
y	9	-4					-9

Solution

a To find *y*, add the two middle lines together.

x	−3	−2	−1	0	1	2	3
6*x*	−18	−12	−6	0	6	12	18
−*x*³	+27	+8	+1	0	−1	−8	−27
y	9	−4	−5	0	5	4	−9

b

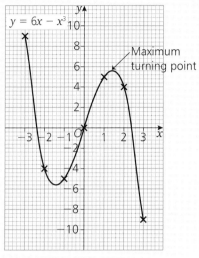

c The maximum turning point is at (1.4, 5.6).

d To solve f(*x*) = 0, look to see where the curve crosses the *x*-axis or f(*x*) = 0.

Solutions are −2.4, 0 and 2.4.

Practise 8.1 – 8.3

1 10 Swiss francs (CHF) = 8.2 euros (EUR)

a Use this information to draw a graph converting between Swiss francs and euros.

b Use your conversion graph to convert 4.5 Swiss francs to euros.

c Explain how you could use the graph to convert 27 Swiss francs to euros.

2 This is the speed–time graph of a three-hour truck journey.

a Find the acceleration of the truck between 14 00 and 14 30.

b What is happening between 15 30 and 16 30?

c Find the deceleration of the truck between 16 30 and 17 00.

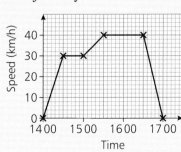

3 a Find the equation of the line through P and Q.

b PQR is a straight line and Q is the midpoint of PR.

Work out the coordinates of R.

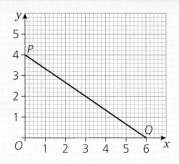

4 a Copy and complete the table of values for $y = 2x^2 + x - 6$.

x	-3	-2	-1	0	1	2	3
$2x^2$	18		2			8	18
y	9		-5			4	15

b Draw the graph of $y = 2x^2 + x - 6$ for values of x from -3 to 3.

c Use your graph to solve the equation $2x^2 + x - 6 = 0$.

d By drawing a suitable line, estimate the gradient of the graph at the point where $x = 1$.

5 $f(x) = \dfrac{2}{x}$ and $g(x) = \dfrac{2x + 1}{2}$

a Draw the graph of $y = f(x)$ for values of x from -3 to 3 $(x \neq 0)$.

b On the same grid, draw the graph of $y = g(x)$.

c Use your graphs to write down estimates of the two solutions of the equation $f(x) = g(x)$.

Transformations

Learning outcomes

After this chapter you should be able to:

- recognise line symmetry in two dimensional (2-D) shapes and draw lines of symmetry
- recognise rotational symmetry in two dimensional (2-D). shapes and find the order of rotational symmetry
- use symmetrical properties of triangles, quadrilaterals, circles and polygons
- use the following transformations of the plane: reflection, rotation, translation, enlargement and their combinations
- identify and give precise descriptions of transformations.

Revise 9.1 Symmetry

Symmetry

Line symmetry

A shape has line symmetry when it can be folded so that one half fits *exactly* over the other. The **line of symmetry** is like a mirror line where each side of the shape is reflected at the other side.

Rotational symmetry

A shape has **rotational symmetry** if it *looks exactly the same* when it is rotated by less than 360° to a *new* position. The **order of rotational symmetry** is the number of different positions in which it looks the same during a complete turn.

Special shapes and their symmetries

The symmetries of some special shapes are shown below:

Equilateral triangle	Isosceles triangle	Scalene triangle
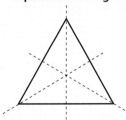	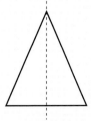	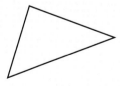
3 lines of symmetry Rotational symmetry of order 3	1 line of symmetry No rotational symmetry (order 1)	No lines of symmetry No rotational symmetry (order 1)

Square

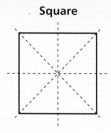

4 lines of symmetry
Rotational symmetry
of order 4

Rectangle

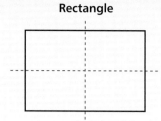

2 lines of symmetry
Rotational symmetry
of order 2

Rhombus

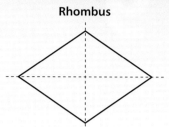

2 lines of symmetry
Rotational symmetry
of order 2

Parallelogram

No lines of symmetry
Rotational symmetry of
order 2

Trapezium

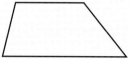

No lines of symmetry
No rotational symmetry
(order 1)

Kite

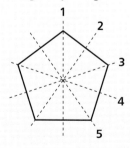

1 line of symmetry
No rotational symmetry
(order 1)

Circle

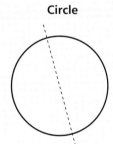

Every diameter of a circle
is a line of symmetry.
It looks the same when
rotated through any angle.

A circle has an infinite number of lines of symmetry.
The order of its rotational symmetry is also infinite.

Regular pentagon

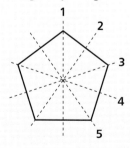

5 lines of symmetry
Rotational symmetry
of order 5

Regular hexagon

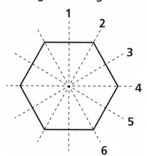

6 lines of symmetry
Rotational symmetry
of order 6

Regular octagon

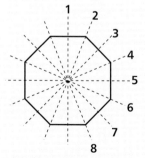

8 lines of symmetry
Rotational symmetry
of order 8

In general, a regular n-sided polygon has n lines of symmetry and rotational symmetry of order n.

Worked examples

Recognising symmetry

a

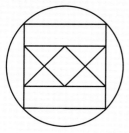

b

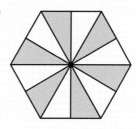

For each diagram, write down: **i** the order of rotational symmetry

ii the number of lines of symmetry.

Solution

a **i** This diagram looks the same if you rotate it by 180°.

It has rotational symmetry of order 2.

ii The diagram has 2 lines of symmetry.

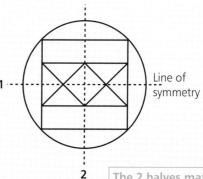

> **Exam tip**
>
> Remember that you can use tracing paper to find or check the answers in transformation or symmetry questions.

The 2 halves match if you fold along either of these lines.

b **i** This diagram has rotational symmetry of order 6.

ii It is not possible to fold this diagram so that the two halves match.

The diagram has no lines of symmetry.

Using symmetry

a A triangle has one line of symmetry.

i What is the geometrical name of this triangle?

ii One angle of the triangle is 100°. Find the other angles.

b A quadrilateral has two parallel sides and one line of symmetry.

One angle of the quadrilateral is 100°. Find the other angles.

Solution

a **i** A triangle with one line of symmetry is an isosceles triangle.

ii The angle sum of a triangle is 180°, so there can only be one angle of 100°.

The sum of the other 2 angles must be 80°.

Each angle = 80° ÷ 2 = 40°

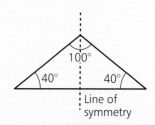

b The line of symmetry means there must be another angle of 100°.

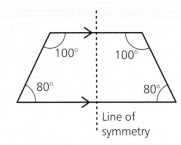

You can check the angles by adding them – the angles of the quadrilateral should add up to 360°.

Line of symmetry

The sum of interior angles on parallel lines is 180°, so the other two angles are both 80°.

Revise 9.2 Reflections, rotations and translations

Reflection

In a **reflection**, each point on the **object** is mapped onto a point on the **image** that is on the other side of the **mirror line**. The object and image points are an equal distance from the mirror line.

On this grid, flag F is mapped onto flag A by a reflection in the x-axis.
Reflection in $x = 4$ maps F onto B.

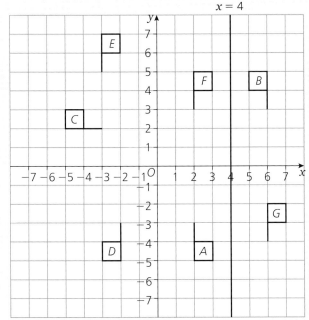

Rotation

In a **rotation**, the object is rotated clockwise or anticlockwise around a **centre of rotation**.

An anticlockwise rotation is identified as a positive angle, and a clockwise rotation as a negative angle. So a rotation of $-90°$ means 90° clockwise.

Flag F is mapped onto flag C by a rotation of 90° anticlockwise (or 270° clockwise) about the origin, (0, 0). A rotation of 180° clockwise or anticlockwise about (4, 0) maps A onto B.

Translation

In a **translation**, the object moves across the page without being rotated or reflected. The translation is sometimes described by a **vector**.

A translation by vector $\begin{pmatrix} -5 \\ 2 \end{pmatrix}$, maps F onto E. A translation by vector $\begin{pmatrix} 4 \\ -7 \end{pmatrix}$, maps F onto G.

The top number in the vector gives the horizontal movement with positive being right and negative left. The bottom number gives the vertical movement with positive being up and negative down.

Worked examples

Reflections

A triangle A has vertices at $(-5, 4)$, $(-1, 6)$ and $(-6, 8)$.

a Reflect triangle A in the line $y = 4$. Label the new shape B.

b Reflect triangle A in the line $x = -2$. Label the new shape C.

c Reflect triangle A in the line $y = x$. Label the new shape D.

Solution

Triangle A is shown on the grid.

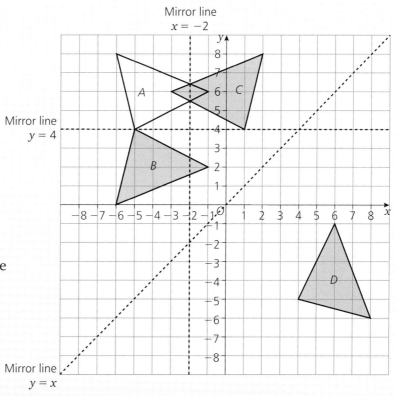

a The mirror line, $y = \mathbf{4}$, goes through points such as $(-1, \mathbf{4})$, $(0, \mathbf{4})$, $(1, \mathbf{4})$ and $(2, \mathbf{4})$.

Reflecting each vertex of triangle A in this mirror line gives triangle B.

b The mirror line, $x = -\mathbf{2}$, goes through points such as $(-\mathbf{2}, -1)$, $(-\mathbf{2}, 0)$, $(-\mathbf{2}, 1)$ and $(-\mathbf{2}, 2)$.

Reflecting each vertex of triangle A in this mirror line gives triangle C.

c The mirror line, $y = x$ is the line through points such as $(-8, -8)$, $(-4, -4)$, $(0, 0)$, $(4, 4)$ and $(8, 8)$.

Reflecting each vertex of triangle A in this mirror line gives triangle D.

$x = -2$ is parallel to the y-axis.
$y = 4$ is parallel to the x-axis.
$y = x$ is a diagonal line as shown.

Exam tip

Remember that if a is a constant then:

- a line with equation $x = a$ is parallel to the y-axis.

- a line with equation $y = a$ is parallel to the x-axis.

The y-axis is also the line $x = 0$.

The x-axis is also the line $y = 0$.

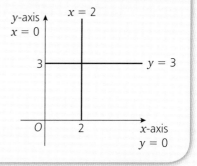

Rotations

Kite K has vertices at $(0, -1)$, $(2, 1)$, $(4, -1)$ and $(2, -5)$.

a Rotate kite K 90° clockwise about the point $(2, -5)$.

Label the new shape A.

b Rotate kite K 180° clockwise about the point $(3, 0)$.

Label the new shape B.

c Rotate kite K 270° anticlockwise about the point $(2, 4)$.

Label the new shape C.

Solution

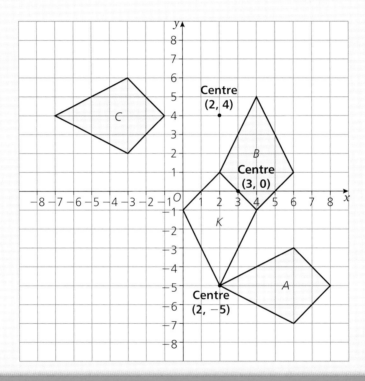

Exam tip

Remember that you can use tracing paper to find or check your answers.

Translations

a On axes for $0 \leqslant x \leqslant 10$ and $0 \leqslant y \leqslant 8$, join points $(2, 3)$, $(3, 3)$, $(4, 4)$, $(3, 5)$ and $(1, 4)$ to give a pentagon P.

b Translate P by vector $\binom{6}{3}$. Label the new shape Q.

c Translate Q by vector $\binom{-2}{-5}$. Label the new shape R.

d Describe the single translation which maps the new shape R onto the original pentagon P.

Solution

a The axes and pentagon *P* are as shown.

b The translation by vector $\begin{pmatrix} 6 \\ 3 \end{pmatrix}$ moves the pentagon, *P*,
6 units to the right and 3 units upwards.

This gives pentagon *Q*.

c The translation by vector $\begin{pmatrix} -2 \\ -5 \end{pmatrix}$ moves *Q* by 2 units to
the left and 5 units downwards to *R*.

d The movement from *R* to *P* is 4 units to the left and
2 units upwards.

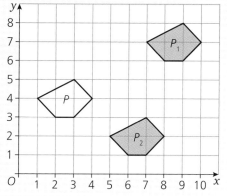

So *R* is mapped onto the original pentagon *P* by a translation by vector $\begin{pmatrix} -4 \\ 2 \end{pmatrix}$.

Revise 9.3 Enlargements

Enlargement

In an **enlargement**, the original shape is enlarged by a **scale factor**.

- When the scale factor is greater than 1, the new shape is bigger than the original shape.
- When the scale factor is between 0 and 1, the new shape is smaller than the original shape.
- When the scale factor equals 1, the new shape is the same size as the original shape.

The lines joining corresponding points on the original shape and the new shape all meet at the
centre of enlargement.

To find a vertex of the new shape,
multiply the distance from the
centre to the original vertex
by the scale factor.

Triangle *T* is mapped onto *A* by an
enlargement with centre $(-7, 1)$
and scale factor 2.

T is mapped onto *B* by an enlargement
with centre $(-1, -5)$ and scale factor $\frac{1}{2}$.

B is mapped onto *A* by an enlargement
with centre $(-3, -3)$ and scale factor 4.

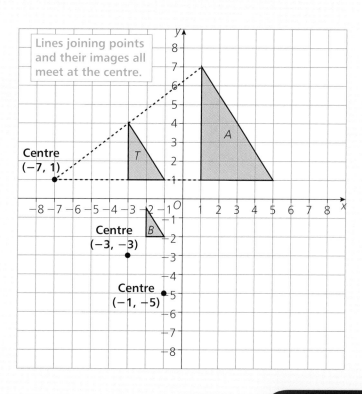

Describing and combining transformations

To describe a **transformation** *fully*, give all the details listed in the table.

To describe a:	You must give:
reflection	the position of the mirror line
rotation	the angle of rotation the direction (clockwise or anticlockwise) the centre of rotation
translation	the vector (or the distance and direction)
enlargement	the scale factor the centre of enlargement

Exam tip

- For *full* marks in the exam you must give a *full* description.
- When asked to describe a single transformation equivalent to a combination of transformations, describing more than one transformation will be awarded no marks.

Worked examples

Enlargements

A parallelogram has vertices at $P(1, 2)$, $Q(3, 2)$, $R(4, 3)$ and $S(2, 3)$.

a Enlarge $PQRS$ by scale factor 3 and centre P.

Label the new shape $P_1Q_1R_1S_1$.

b Find the ratio of the area of $PQRS$ to the area of $P_1Q_1R_1S_1$, giving your answer in its simplest form.

Solution

a The centre of the enlargement, P, does not move in the enlargement.

The distance from P to each of the other vertices is multiplied by 3.

Joining these image points gives the parallelogram $P_1Q_1R_1S_1$.

b The ratio of lengths in $PQRS$ to lengths in $P_1Q_1R_1S_1$ is $1 : 3$.

$P_1Q_1R_1S_1$ is similar to $PQRS$, so the ratio of the area of $PQRS$ to the area of $P_1Q_1R_1S_1$ is $1 : 3^2 = 1 : 9$.

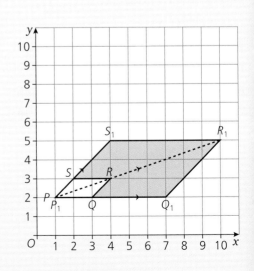

Exam tip

Always try to use the
quickest method. If
you have time, use an
alternative method to
check your answer.

You can check the ratios by finding the area of each parallelogram:

Area of $PQRS$ = base × height = 2 × 1 = 2 square units.

Area of $P_1Q_1R_1S_1$ = 6 × 3 = 18 square units.

The ratio of the area of $PQRS$ to the area of $P_1Q_1R_1S_1$ = 2 : 18 = 1 : 9.

Combining transformations

Triangle T has vertices at $(-4, 1)$, $(-4, 3)$ and $(-3, 3)$.

a Use axes with $-5 \leqslant x \leqslant 5$ and $-1 \leqslant y \leqslant 5$, rotate T 90° clockwise about the origin. Label the new shape U.

b Reflect U in the line $y = x$. Label the new shape V.

c Describe fully the single transformation that maps T onto V.

Solution

a Rotating T through 90° clockwise about the origin gives U.

b Reflecting U in the line $y = x$ then gives V.

c The single transformation which maps T onto V is reflection in the y-axis (or $x = 0$ line).

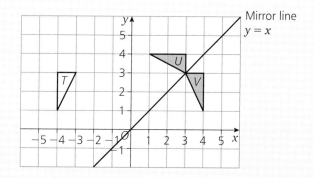

Describing transformations

a Describe fully the transformation that maps the letter F to:

  i shaded shape A

  ii shaded shape B

b Describe fully the transformation that maps the letter L to:

  i shaded shape P

  ii shaded shape Q

  iii shaded shape R

  iv shaded shape S.

Exam tip

For *full marks* you must
give a *full* description.

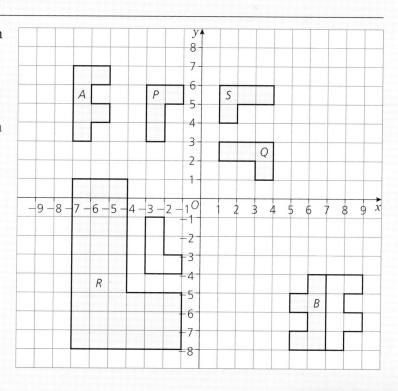

Solution

a **i** The letter F moves 14 units to the left and 11 units upwards to give shaded *A*.

The transformation is a translation by vector $\begin{pmatrix} -14 \\ 11 \end{pmatrix}$.

ii The letter F is rotated through a half turn to give shaded shape *B*.

The point $(7, -6)$ stays in place, so this is the centre of the rotation.

The transformation is a rotation of 180° clockwise (or anticlockwise) about the point $(7, -6)$.

b **i** The letter L is reflected in the line $y = 1$ to give shaded shape *P*.

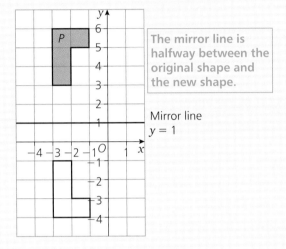

The mirror line is halfway between the original shape and the new shape.

Mirror line $y = 1$

ii The letter L is reflected in the line $y = -x$ to give shaded shape *Q*.

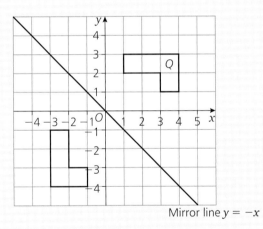

You can check by tracing and folding along the mirror line.

Mirror line $y = -x$

iii The sides of shaded shape *R* are three times the lengths of the sides of the letter L.

The transformation is an enlargement with centre $(-1, -2)$ and scale factor 3.

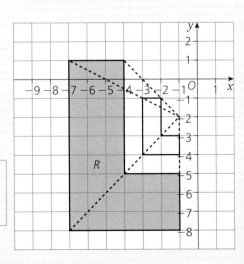

To find the centre, draw lines joining each vertex of the original shape and the new shape.

iv The transformation that maps the letter L onto shaded shape *S* is a rotation of 90° clockwise (or 270° anticlockwise) about the point (4, −1).

> Use tracing paper or perpendicular bisectors to find the centre.

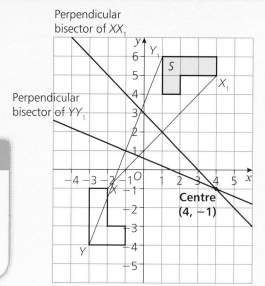

Exam tip

To find a difficult centre of rotation, draw the perpendicular bisectors of lines joining points and their images. The perpendicular bisectors meet at the centre of rotation.

When describing fully a single transformation, mentioning more than one transformation will score 0 marks.

Practise 9.1 – 9.3

1 For each diagram below, write down:

   i the number of lines of symmetry   **ii** the order of rotational symmetry.

a 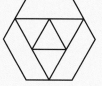 **b**  **c**   **d**

2 Make two copies of this diagram.

  a On the first copy, shade one more square so that there is one line of symmetry.

  b On the second copy, shade two more squares so that there is rotational symmetry of order 2.

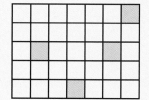

3 a Quadrilateral *A* has rotational symmetry of order 2, but no lines of symmetry.

   i Sketch quadrilateral *A* and write down its geometrical name.

   ii Mark on your sketch the equal sides and angles of the shape.

   iii One angle of quadrilateral *A* is 50°. Find the sizes of the other angles.

  b Quadrilateral *B* has 1 line of symmetry, but no rotational symmetry.

   The diagonals of quadrilateral *B* are not equal in length.

   i Sketch quadrilateral *B* and write down its geometrical name.

   ii Mark on your sketch the equal sides and angles of the shape.

   iii Quadrilateral *B* has two angles of 105°.
   One of the remaining angles is twice the size of the other. Find the sizes of these angles.

4 a On axes of x and y from -8 to 8, draw the quadrilateral with vertices at $(2, 4)$, $(4, 4)$, $(4, 5)$ and $(1, 6)$. Label the quadrilateral A.

   b Reflect A in the line $y = -1$. Label the new shape B.

   c Reflect A in the line $x = -2$. Label the new shape C.

   d Rotate A through 90° clockwise about the origin. Label the new shape D.

   e Rotate A through 180° clockwise about the point $(4, 4)$. Label the new shape E.

   f Translate A by vector $\begin{pmatrix} 4 \\ 2 \end{pmatrix}$. Label the new shape F.

   g Translate A by vector $\begin{pmatrix} -8 \\ -7 \end{pmatrix}$. Label the new shape G.

   h Enlarge A with centre $(4, 7)$ and scale factor 3. Label the new shape H.

5 Describe fully the single transformation which maps:

   a A onto B

   b A onto C

   c A onto D

   d B onto E

   e B onto H

   f F onto G

   g H onto I

   h D onto G

   i I onto J

   j E onto K.

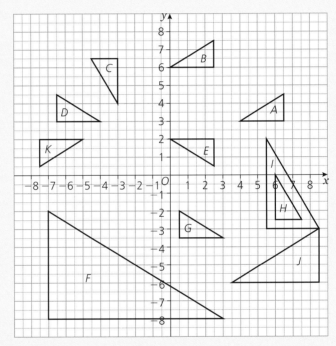

6 On axes of x and y from -7 to 7, draw the kite with vertices at $A(2, 1)$, $B(1, 0)$, $C(2, -3)$ and $D(3, 0)$.

   a Enlarge $ABCD$ with scale factor 2 and centre A. Label the new shape $A_1B_1C_1D_1$.

   b Find the ratio, area of $ABCD$: area of $A_1B_1C_1D_1$ in its simplest form.

7 a On axes of x and y from -6 to 6 draw:

    i the square $ABCD$ with vertices $A(-2, 2)$, $B(0, 4)$, $C(-2, 6)$ and $D(-4, 4)$

    ii the square $PQRS$ with vertices $P(4, -4)$, $Q(6, -2)$, $R(4, 0)$ and $S(2, -2)$.

   b Describe fully the single transformation which maps:

    i $ABCD$ onto $PQRS$ (remember the order of the letters is important: A must map onto P, B onto Q, C onto R and D onto S)

    ii $ABCD$ onto $QRSP$

    iii $ABCD$ onto $RSPQ$

    iv $ABCD$ onto $SPQR$

    v $ABCD$ onto $SRQP$.

8 Trapezium T has vertices at $(5, 2)$, $(8, 2)$, $(7, 4)$ and $(5, 4)$.

   a Using axes with $-8 \leqslant x \leqslant 8$ and $-5 \leqslant y \leqslant 5$, draw and label T.

   b Reflect T in the line $x = 3$. Label the new shape U.

   c Reflect U in the line $y = -x$. Label the new shape V.

   d Describe fully the single transformation that maps T onto V.

9 For this question use axes of x and y from -8 to 8.

  Q is the quadrilateral with vertices at $(2, 2)$, $(3, 2)$, $(5, 5)$ and $(2, 4)$.

   a Reflect Q in the x-axis and label the new shape R.

   b Rotate R clockwise through $90°$ about the origin. Label the new shape S.

   c Describe fully a single transformation which maps Q onto S

   d Rotate Q clockwise through $90°$ about the point $(2, -1)$. Label the new shape T.

   e Translate T by the vector $\begin{pmatrix} -9 \\ 5 \end{pmatrix}$. Label the new shape U.

   f Describe fully a single transformation which maps Q onto U.

10 More number

Learning outcomes

After this chapter you should be able to:

- round numbers to 10, 100, … or to a specified number of decimal places or significant figures
- give appropriate upper and lower bounds for data to a specified degree of accuracy and use these in calculations
- calculate squares, square roots, cubes and cube roots of numbers
- use and interpret positive, negative and zero and fractional indices and use the rules of indices
- use prime factors to find lowest common multiples and highest common factors
- use and convert to and from standard form
- use language, notation and Venn diagrams to describe sets and represent relationships between sets
- define a set in a variety of ways
- understand and use set notation
- manipulate surds.

Revise 10.1 Estimation and accuracy

Rounding

Whole numbers

Numbers can be **rounded** to the nearest **integer** (whole number) or to the nearest power of 10, e.g. 10, 100 or 1000.

To round to the nearest 10, for example, look at the number in the next place value (units) column.

Round *up* if this number is 5 or more.

Round *down* if this number is less than 5.

So 328 would be rounded up to 330, but 324 would be rounded down to 320.

Similarly, to round to the nearest 100, look in the tens column, and to round to the nearest 1000, look in the hundreds column.

Numbers can also be rounded to a given number of decimal places or **significant figures**.

Decimal places

Decimal places are counted from the right of the decimal point.

To round to 2 decimal places, for example, look at the 3rd decimal place.

If this digit is 5 or more, round *up*.

If this digit is less than 5, round *down*.

Exam tip

Rounding to 1 decimal place is the same as rounding to the nearest tenth.

Rounding to 2 decimal places is the same as rounding to the nearest hundredth.

Rounding to 3 decimal places is the same as rounding to the nearest thousandth.

Significant figures

Significant figures are counted from the first non-zero digit, ignoring the position of the decimal point.

Ignore any zeros at the front of the number as they are not significant.

For example,

Rounding 236.5396 to the nearest hundredth gives

236.53|96 = 236.54 (to the nearest hundredth) ⟵————————— Round up

Rounding 236.5396 to 4 significant figures gives

236.5|396 = 236.5 (to 4 s.f.)

Rounding 236.5396 to 3 decimal places gives

236.539|6 = 236.540 (to 3 d.p.) ⟵————————— Round up

You must show 3 decimal places so fill in the third place with a zero.

Estimating

When using a calculator to find the answers, it is useful to estimate your answer first.

This is usually done by rounding each number to 1 significant figure.

This estimate should be close to your calculated answer. It often shows you quickly if you have made a mistake by entering numbers incorrectly or pressing the wrong calculator key.

Upper and lower bounds

The **upper** and **lower bounds** are the maximum and the minimum values of the number before rounding.

When a number has been rounded, you can work backwards to find the numbers it could have been before rounding.

For example, a number has been rounded to the nearest centimetre. You can find the upper and lower bounds by taking half of this (0.5 cm) and adding it to and subtracting it from the number.

When you are given a number that has been rounded, and have not been told to what it has been rounded, then always give your answer to the next degree of accuracy.

For example, 34.24 has been given to 2 decimal places or 4 significant figures. The upper and lower bounds should be given to 3 decimal places or 5 significant figures.

Watch out for ambiguous questions where the rounded value gives you no indication as to how it has been rounded, e.g. 27 000 could have been rounded to the nearest 1000, to the nearest 100, to the nearest 10 or to the nearest unit.

> **Exam tip**
>
> In the examination, you are sometimes asked to give the answers as inequalities.
>
> For example:
>
> minimum length $\leqslant$ length $<$ maximum length
>
> 14.75 cm $\leqslant$ length $<$ 14.85 cm
>
> Notice the two different inequalities used. The maximum length itself cannot be reached but you still refer to this as the upper bound.

Upper and lower bounds in calculations

You must be able to use upper and lower bounds in calculations involving addition, subtraction, multiplication and division. You will then be asked to find the overall maximum and minimum values.

When adding:

overall maximum = upper bound of A + upper bound of B

overall minimum = lower bound of A + lower bound of B

When subtracting:

overall maximum = upper bound of A − lower bound of B

overall minimum = lower bound of A − upper bound of B

When multiplying:

overall maximum = upper bound of A × upper bound of B

overall minimum = lower bound of A × lower bound of B

When dividing:

$$\text{overall maximum} = \frac{\text{upper bound of A}}{\text{lower bound of B}}$$

$$\text{overall minimum} = \frac{\text{lower bound of A}}{\text{upper bound of B}}$$

When substituting into formulae or calculations involving more than one operation, you will need to think carefully about how to combine the upper and lower bounds.

Worked examples

Estimating

$$\frac{472 \times 0.247}{0.98 + 1.492}$$

a Estimate the value of this calculation.

b Use your calculator to find the value of the original calculation correct to 3 significant figures.

Solution

a $\dfrac{4|72 \times 0.2|47}{0.9|8 + 1|.492}$

Round each number correct to 1 significant figure.

This gives:

$$\frac{500 \times 0.2}{1 + 1}$$

$$= \frac{100}{2}$$

$$= 50$$

b $\dfrac{472 \times 0.247}{0.98 + 1.492}$

$$= 47.1|618123...$$

$$= 47.2 \text{ (to 3 s.f.)}$$

Upper and lower bounds

The Sydney Harbour Bridge is 1149 metres in length (to the nearest metre).

a Copy and complete the following statement:

____ m ⩽ length < ____ m

b This bridge is said to be the tallest bridge of its kind in the world. It measures 134 metres from the top of the bridge to the level of the water.

If this height had been measured to the nearest 0.5 metre, copy and complete the following statement:

____ cm ⩽ height < ____ cm

Solution

a The length of the bridge has been rounded to the nearest metre.

So the upper and lower bounds are half of this, 0.5 m, to each side of 1149 m.

The upper bound is 1149 + 0.5 = 1149.5 m.

The lower bound is 1149 − 0.5 = 1148.5 m.

So

1148.5 m ⩽ length < 1.149.5 m

b The height of the bridge has been rounded to the nearest 0.5 m.

The answer is required in centimetres so 134 m = 13 400 cm.

100 cm = 1 m

So the upper and lower bounds are half of this, 0.25 m or 25 cm, to each side of 13 400 cm.

The upper bound is 13 400 + 25 = 13 425 cm.

The lower bound is 13 400 − 25 = 13 375 cm.

So

13 375 cm ⩽ height < 13 425 cm

Calculating with upper and lower bounds

A moving walkway at the airport is 358 metres long, correct to 3 significant figures.

It moves at a speed of 2.4 metres per second, correct to 1 decimal place.

a Write down the upper and lower bounds for:

   i the length of the walkway   **ii** the speed of the walkway.

b Use your answers from part **a** to complete the inequality for the maximum and minimum possible times taken for a piece of luggage to travel from one end of the walkway to the other.

         _____ seconds $\leqslant$ time $<$ _____ seconds

Give your answers to the nearest second.

Solution

a **i** The length has been rounded to 3 significant figures, so

       upper bound = 358.5 metres   lower bound = 357.5 metres

   ii The speed of the walkway has been rounded to 1 decimal place, so

       upper bound = 2.45 metres per second   lower bound = 2.35 metres per second

b Time (in seconds) $= \dfrac{\text{length (in metres)}}{\text{speed (in metres per second)}}$

      Maximum time $= \dfrac{\text{maximum length}}{\text{minimum speed}}$

                  $= \dfrac{358.5}{2.35}$ seconds

                  $= 152.55319...$ seconds

                  $= 153$ seconds or 2 minutes and 33 seconds (to the nearest second)

      Minimum time $= \dfrac{\text{minimum length}}{\text{maximum speed}}$

                  $= \dfrac{357.5}{2.45}$ seconds

                  $= 145.91836...$ seconds

                  $= 146$ seconds or 2 minutes and 26 seconds (to the nearest second)

        146 seconds $\leqslant$ time $<$ 153 seconds

Revise 10.2 Indices and standard form

Squares and cubes

Squares and square roots

A **square number** is the number you get when you multiply a number by itself, e.g. $7 \times 7 = 49$.

It can be written in **index notation** as 7^2.

The opposite or **inverse** of squaring is finding the **square root**.

$7^2 = 49$ so $\sqrt{49} = 7$ or -7

However the $\sqrt{}$ sign usually means find the positive square root.

Cubes and cube roots

A **cube number** is the number you get when you multiply three of the same number together,

e.g. $4 \times 4 \times 4 = 64$.

It can be written in index notation as 4^3.

The opposite or inverse of cubing is finding the **cube root**.

$$4^3 = 4 \times 4 \times 4 = 64, \text{ so } \sqrt[3]{64} = 4$$

Indices and powers

Index form can also be used to show higher powers than 2 or 3:

$$6^5 = 6 \times 6 \times 6 \times 6 \times 6$$

The **index** or **power** tells you how many times the **base number** has to be multiplied by itself.

Index (or power)

3^4

Base number

You say this as '3 to the power of 4'.

3^4 means $3 \times 3 \times 3 \times 3 = 81$.

When finding a root of a number other than 2 or 3 on a calculator, use one of the following keys:

The rules of indices

1. When *multiplying* powers of the same number, *add* the indices:

    $$a^m \times a^n = a^{m+n}$$

2. When *dividing* powers of the same number, *subtract* the indices:

    $$a^m \div a^n = a^{m-n}$$

3. To *raise a power* of a number to another power, *multiply* the indices:

    $$(a^m)^n = a^{m \times n}$$

Negative indices

Negative indices can be written as the corresponding positive index of the reciprocal:

$$a^{-n} = \frac{1}{a^n}$$

Zero indices

Zero indices always have a value of 1:

$$a^0 = 1 \qquad \text{The exception is } 0^0 \text{ which is not defined.}$$

Fractional indices

Fractional indices involve finding roots of numbers:

$$a^{\frac{1}{n}} = \sqrt[n]{a}$$

and $\qquad a^{\frac{m}{n}} = \sqrt[n]{a^m} \text{ or } (\sqrt[n]{a})^m$

Prime factors

The **prime factors** of a number are the prime numbers that multiply together to make that number.

To find the prime factors of a number, divide it by any prime numbers that leave no remainder until the answer is 1.

For example, to find the prime factors of 140:

```
        1
  7 ) 7
  5 ) 35
  2 ) 70
  2 ) 140
```

The prime factors of 140 are 2, 2, 5 and 7. ←——— Note that the order does not matter.

140, written as the product of its prime factors, in index form is $2^2 \times 5 \times 7$.

Using prime factors to find a highest common factor and a lowest common multiple

As the product of their prime factors,

$140 = 2 \times 2 \qquad \times 5 \times 7$

$315 = \qquad 3 \times 3 \times 5 \times 7$

$\qquad\qquad 5 \times 7 \qquad$ are the common factors.

So $\qquad 5 \times 7 = 35 \qquad$ is the highest common factor of 140 and 315.

$140 = 2 \times 2 \qquad \times 5 \times 7$

$315 = \qquad 3 \times 3 \times 5 \times 7$

$2 \times 2 \times 3 \times 3 \times 5 \times 7 \qquad$ contains all the factors of 140 and 315.

$2 \times 2 \times 3 \times 3 \times 5 \times 7 = 1260$

So 1260 is the lowest common multiple of 140 and 315.

Standard form

A number is in **standard form** if it is written in the form:

A power of 10 where n is an integer.

$$A \times 10^n$$

$1 \leqslant A < 10$

Standard form is used to write down very large and very small numbers. This makes them easier to use when doing calculations.

> **Exam tip**
>
> Large numbers, when rewritten in standard form, will always be multiplied by a positive power of 10. Small numbers, when rewritten in standard form, will always be multiplied by a negative power of 10. Make sure you know how to enter numbers in standard form into your calculator.

Converting to standard form

You should make sure that you can convert an ordinary number into standard form and a number in standard form back to an ordinary number.

Adding, subtracting, multiplying and dividing numbers in standard form

When calculating with numbers in standard form, you may need to use the rules of indices mentioned earlier.

> **Exam tip**
>
> When calculating with numbers in standard form, it is useful to put brackets around the number. This makes it easier to see what you are doing, e.g. $(5 \times 10^3) \times (3 \times 10^4)$.

Worked examples

Indices

Simplify:

a $6p^3 \times 2p^{-2}$ **b** $15q^2 \div 5q^{-3}$ **c** $(2r^{-3})^2$ **d** $\left(\frac{27}{125}x^{21}\right)^{\frac{1}{3}}$ **e** $\frac{(16p^8)^{\frac{1}{2}} \times 2p^{-1}}{64p^{\frac{2}{3}}}$

Solution

Always deal with the whole numbers separately from the indices.

a $6p^3 \times 2p^{-2} = 12p^{3+(-2)} = 12p^{3-2} = 12p$ ⟵ Using the 1st rule of indices.

b $15q^2 \div 5q^{-3} = \frac{15}{5}q^{2-(-3)} = 3q^{2+3} = 3q^5$ ⟵ Using the 2nd rule of indices.

c $(2r^{-3})^2 = (2^2)(r^{-3})^2 = 4r^{-3\times2} = 4r^{-6}$ or $\dfrac{4}{r^6}$ ← Using the 3rd rule of indices.

d $\left(\dfrac{27}{125}x^{21}\right)^{\frac{1}{3}} = \dfrac{(27)^{\frac{1}{3}}}{(125)^{\frac{1}{3}}}(x^{21})^{\frac{1}{3}}$ ← By treating each part separately.

$= \dfrac{\sqrt[3]{27}}{\sqrt[3]{125}}x^{21\times\frac{1}{3}}$ ← Using the rule for fractional indices.

$= \dfrac{3}{5}x^7$ ← Using the third rule of indices.

e $\dfrac{(16p^8)^{\frac{1}{2}}\times2p^{-1}}{64p^{\frac{2}{3}}} = \dfrac{4p^4\times2p^{-1}}{64p^{\frac{2}{3}}} = \dfrac{8p^3}{64p^{\frac{2}{3}}} = \dfrac{1}{8}p^{3-\frac{2}{3}} = \dfrac{1}{8}p^{\frac{7}{3}}$

Standard form

a Write the following two numbers in standard form:

789 000 000 and 0.000543

b Calculate the following, giving your answers in standard form:

i $(7.2\times10^4)\times(5\times10^{-3})$

ii $(6.5\times10^4)+(3.2\times10^3)$

Solution

a 789 000 000 ← 7.89 is between 1 and 10.

$= 7.89\times10^8$ ← To get from 789 000 000 to 7.89, the number has moved 8 places right.

0.000543 ← 5.43 is between 1 and 10.

$= 5.43\times10^{-4}$ ← To get from 0.000543 to 5.43, the number has moved 4 places left.

b You may use a calculator to find these answers, but the solutions below show how they can be found without a calculator.

i $(7.2\times10^4)\times(5\times10^{-3})$

$= 7.2\times5\times10^4\times10^{-3}$ ← Multiply the first part of each number together.

$= 36\times10^{4+(-3)}$ ← Use the 1st rule of indices.

$= 36\times10^1$

$= 3.6\times10^1\times10^1$ ← Write 36 as 3.6×10^1.

$= 3.6\times10^2$ ← Use the 1st rule of indices again.

ii $(6.5\times10^4)+(3.2\times10^3)$

$= 65\,000+3200$

$= 68\,200$

$= 6.82\times10^4$ ← Write 68 200 in standard form.

Using standard form in calculations

A particular pine tree pollen consists of minute spherical grains each 55 micrometres (μm) in diameter.

$$1 \text{ micrometre} = 1 \times 10^{-6} \text{ metres}$$

a Write down the diameter of a grain in metres.

b Find the volume of 200 of these grains in micrometres cubed (μm^3).

c Convert the answer to part **b** into a volume in m^3.

Give all your answers in standard form correct to 3 significant figures.

Solution

a 55 micrometres $= 55 \times 10^{-6} = 5.5 \times 10^{-5}$ metre

b Volume of a sphere $= \frac{4}{3}\pi r^3$ <---------------------- Radius $= 27.5\,\mu m$

$$= \frac{4}{3} \times \pi \times 27.5^3 \,\mu\text{m}^3$$

$$= 87114 \,\mu\text{m}^3 \text{ (to the nearest } \mu\text{m}^3)$$

Volume of 200 spheres $= 200 \times 87\,114 \,\mu\text{m}^3$

$$= 17\,422\,800 \,\mu\text{m}^3$$

$$= 1.74 \times 10^7 \,\mu\text{m}^3 \text{ (to 3 s.f.)}$$

c $1\,\mu\text{m} = 1 \times 10^{-6}\,\text{m}$

So $1\,\mu\text{m}^3 = (10^{-6})^3\,\text{m}^3$

Or $1\,\mu\text{m}^3 = 10^{-18}\,\text{m}^3$

So volume of 200 spheres $= 1.74 \times 10^7 \,\mu\text{m}^3$

$$= 1.74 \times 10^7 \times 10^{-18}\,\text{m}^3$$

$$= 1.74 \times 10^{-11}\,\text{m}^3 \text{ (to 3 s.f.)}$$

Prime factors

a Write 135 as the product of its prime factors. Give your answer in index form.

b The battery in a phone needs recharging every 225 hours. The battery in a laptop needs recharging every 135 hours. If I charge them both now, how long will it be until they both need recharging at the same time?

Solution

a

```
          1
   3 )    3
   3 )    9
   3 )   27
   5 )  135
```

The prime factors of 135 are $3^3 \times 5$.

b The number of hours until they both need recharging together is the lowest common multiple of 225 and 135.

```
            1
  3 )   3
  3 )   9
  5 )  45
  5 ) 225
```

$135 = 3 \times 3 \times 3 \times 5$

$225 = 3 \times 3 \quad\ \times 5 \times 5$

$\quad\quad 3 \times 3 \times 3 \times 5 \times 5 = 675$

They will need recharging together after 675 hours.

Revise 10.3 Set notation

Set notation

A **set** is a collection of objects or numbers, usually having something in common.

The members of a set are called the **elements** of the set.

Set notation

A set is named with a capital letter, for example, set A.

The **membership** of the set is all the elements in the set.

The symbol $\in$ means 'is an element of'

$\notin$ means 'is not an element of'.

A set can contain items or numbers.

It can also contain **ordered pairs**. These are pairs that go together, like coordinates.

The members of a set can be listed or defined, for example,

$A = \{1, 2, 3, 4, 6, 12\}$ is the same as $A = \{x : x \text{ is a factor of } 12\}$

This is read as 'A is the set of all elements x such that x is a factor of 12'.

Venn diagrams

A **Venn diagram** is a way of showing the elements of sets in a diagram.

A rectangle represents the **Universal Set**, written as $\mathscr{E}$.

This is the set containing all the elements to be considered.

Other sets are shown as circles.

Combining sets

$\mathscr{E}$ = Universal Set

C is contained in A.

So C is a **subset** of A, or $C \subset A$.

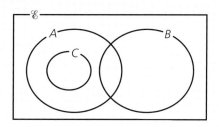

The **union** of A and B, $A \cup B$, is everything in A or B (all of the shaded sections put together).

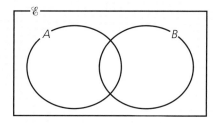

The **intersection** of A and B, $A \cap B$, is everything in *both* A and B (the shaded section).

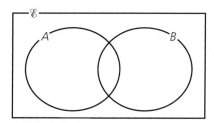

An **empty set**, or **null set**, $\varnothing$, is one that contains no elements.

The **complement** of set A, A', is the set of everything not in set A (the shaded section).

The number of elements in set A is written as n(A)

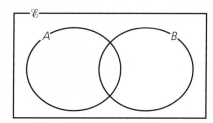

Worked examples

Drawing and interpreting Venn diagrams

$\mathscr{E} = \{x : x \in \text{Natural numbers}, x < 11\}$

$A = \{x : x \text{ is an even number}\}$

$B = \{x : x \text{ is a factor of } 10\}$

$C = \{x : x \text{ is a factor of } 12\}$.

a List the elements of: **i** A **ii** A' **iii** $A \cap B$.

b Show this information in a Venn diagram.

c List the elements of $(A \cup C)'$.

Solution

$\mathcal{E} = \{1, 2, 3, 4, 5, 6, 7, 8, 9, 10\}$

$A = \{2, 4, 6, 8, 10\}$

$B = \{1, 2, 5, 10\}$

$C = \{1, 2, 3, 4, 6\}$

Exam tip

List the elements of each set before drawing the Venn diagram.

a   i $A = \{2, 4, 6, 8, 10\}$ **ii** $A' = \{1, 3, 5, 7, 9\}$ **iii** $A \cap B = \{2, 10\}$

b

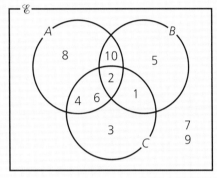

$(A \cup C) = \{1, 2, 3, 4, 6, 8, 10\}$

c So $(A \cup C)' = \{5, 7, 9\}$

Venn diagrams can also be used to show the number of elements in a set.

Number of elements in a set

There are 35 people working in an office.

18 wear glasses (G), 20 wear a watch (W) and 9 wear neither glasses nor a watch.

Show this information on a Venn diagram.

Solution

9 people wear neither glasses nor a watch.

These go outside the glasses and watch circles on the Venn diagram.

So there are $35 - 9 = 26$ in $G \cup W$.

There are 20 in W, so there must be $26 - 20 = 6$ in $G \cap W'$.

So there are $18 - 6 = 12$ in $G \cap W$.

That leaves 8 in $W \cap G'$.

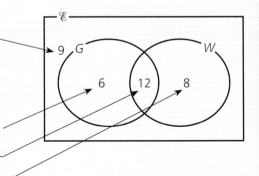

Revise 10.4 Surds

Simplifying surds

A **surd** is an expression containing one or more irrational roots of numbers, such as $2\sqrt{3}$, or $3\sqrt{2} + 6$.

Surds are exact and can be simplified using these rules:

$$(\sqrt{a})^2 = a$$

$$a\sqrt{c} \pm b\sqrt{c} = (a \pm b)\sqrt{c}$$

$$\sqrt{ab} = \sqrt{a} \times \sqrt{b}$$

$$\sqrt{\frac{a}{b}} = \frac{\sqrt{a}}{\sqrt{b}}$$

Simplifying a surd involves reducing the number of terms and reducing the root to the smallest possible number.

$\sqrt{28} = \sqrt{4 \times 7} = \sqrt{4} \times \sqrt{7} = 2 \times \sqrt{7}$, so $2\sqrt{7}$ is the simplest form of $\sqrt{28}$

Expanding brackets and rationalising the denominator

You can expand brackets containing roots just as you do with algebraic expressions.

Square roots can be removed from the denominator of a fraction using $(\sqrt{a})^2 = a$.

Worked examples

Simplifying surds

Simplify:

a $\sqrt{45}$ **b** $\sqrt{10} \times \sqrt{15}$ **c** $\dfrac{\sqrt{40}}{\sqrt{5}}$

Solution

a $\sqrt{45}$

$= \sqrt{9 \times 5}$

$= \sqrt{9} \times \sqrt{5}$

$= 3\sqrt{5}$

b $\sqrt{10} \times \sqrt{15}$

$= \sqrt{10 \times 15}$

$= \sqrt{150}$

$= \sqrt{25 \times 6}$

$= \sqrt{25} \times \sqrt{6}$

$= 5\sqrt{6}$

c $\dfrac{\sqrt{40}}{\sqrt{5}}$

$= \sqrt{\dfrac{40}{5}}$

$= \sqrt{8}$

$= \sqrt{4 \times 2}$

$= \sqrt{4} \times \sqrt{2}$

$= 2\sqrt{2}$

Expanding brackets

Simplify:

a $\sqrt{5}(3 - \sqrt{10})$

b $(3 + \sqrt{5})(2 - \sqrt{5})$

Solution

a $\sqrt{5}(3 - \sqrt{10})$

$= \sqrt{5} \times 3 - \sqrt{5} \times \sqrt{10}$

$= 3\sqrt{5} - \sqrt{50}$

$= 3\sqrt{5} - \sqrt{25 \times 2}$

$= 3\sqrt{5} - 5\sqrt{2}$

b $(3 + \sqrt{5})(2 - \sqrt{5})$

$= 3 \times 2 - 3 \times \sqrt{5} + \sqrt{5} \times 2 - \sqrt{5} \times \sqrt{5}$

$= 6 - 3\sqrt{5} + 2\sqrt{5} - 5$

$= 1 - \sqrt{5}$

Rationalising denominators

Simplify the following by rationalising the denominator:

a $\dfrac{3}{\sqrt{7}}$

b $\dfrac{9}{2\sqrt{3}}$

c $\dfrac{3\sqrt{6}}{5\sqrt{3}}$

Solution

a $\dfrac{3}{\sqrt{7}}$

$= \dfrac{3 \times \sqrt{7}}{\sqrt{7} \times \sqrt{7}}$

$= \dfrac{3\sqrt{7}}{7}$

b $\dfrac{9}{2\sqrt{3}}$

$= \dfrac{9 \times \sqrt{3}}{2\sqrt{3} \times \sqrt{3}}$

$= \dfrac{9\sqrt{3}}{2 \times 3}$

$= \dfrac{3\sqrt{3}}{2}$

c $\dfrac{3\sqrt{6}}{5\sqrt{3}}$

$= \dfrac{3\sqrt{6} \times \sqrt{3}}{5\sqrt{3} \times \sqrt{3}}$

$= \dfrac{3\sqrt{18}}{5 \times 3}$

$= \dfrac{\sqrt{18}}{5}$

$= \dfrac{\sqrt{9 \times 2}}{5} = \dfrac{3\sqrt{2}}{5}$

Practise 10.1 – 10.4

1 $(0.321 + 0.192)^2 \times 438 - \sqrt{3.92}$

   a Write all the numbers in the above calculation correct to 1 significant figure.

   b Use your answers to estimate the value of the calculation.

   c Use your calculator to find the value of the original calculation, correct to 4 significant figures.

2 The population of Shanghai in the 2000 census was assessed at being 16 737 734.

    a Rewrite this population correct to:

        i the nearest 10 000

        ii the nearest 100.

    b In 2010, the population had increased to 23 020 000 (to the nearest ten thousand).

    Copy and complete the following statement:

        _____ ⩽ population < _____

    c The actual population in 2010 was stated as 23 019 148.

    Find the percentage increase in population from 2000 to 2010.

    Give your answer correct to 1 decimal place.

3 The population of Nepal in July 2011 was 2.97×10^7.

The area of Nepal is $1.47 \times 10^5 \, \text{km}^2$.

Work out the average number of people per km^2 in July 2011.

Give your answer as an ordinary number.

4 **a** Write the following ordinary numbers in standard form:

        i 17 400   **ii** 0.005328

    b Write the following numbers, given in standard form, as ordinary numbers:

        i 3.254×10^6 **ii** 3.254×10^{-5}

5 Write each of these four numbers on the Venn diagram:

    3.4 $\sqrt{36}$ $\sqrt{35}$ $\dfrac{5}{\sqrt{9}}$

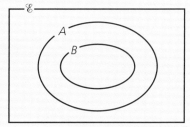

$\mathscr{E}$ = {real numbers}

A = {rational numbers}

B = {integers}

6 To raise money for charity, Fariah walks 28 km (correct to the nearest km). She does this every day for 7 days.

    a Copy and complete the statement below:

        _____ ⩽ distance walked in 1 day < _____

    b Fariah was sponsored for a total of $2.5 per kilometre walked.

    Find the maximum and the minimum amount of money that Fariah had raised at the end of 7 days. Give your answer correct to the nearest dollar.

7 n($\mathscr{E}$) = 35, n(A) = 18, n($A \cap B$) = 7 and n($A' \cap B$) = 6.

Complete the Venn diagram to show this information about the numbers of elements.

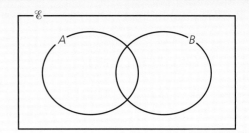

8 $\mathscr{E} = \{x : x \in \mathbb{N}, x \leqslant 12\}$

$A = \{x : x \text{ is a prime number}\}$

$B = \{x : x \text{ is a square number}\}$

$C = \{x : x \text{ is a multiple of 3}\}$

Draw a Venn diagram to show this information.

9 a The diameter of a red blood cell is 7 μm.

1 μm is called a micrometre and is equal to $\dfrac{1}{1\,000\,000}$ metre.

Write down the diameter of the red blood cell in metres and in standard form.

b Use the formula:

$$A = \frac{B^{\frac{3}{2}}}{C^2}$$

to calculate A, when $B = 1.44 \times 10^6$ and $C = 4.8 \times 10^5$.

Give your answer in standard form.

10 On the Venn diagrams, shade the regions:

    a $A' \cap B$ **b** $A' \cup B$.

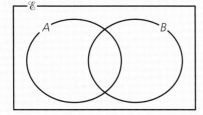 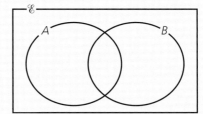

11 a Find the value of p when $3^p \times 3^2 = 3^7$.

    b Find the value of q when $\dfrac{8^q}{8^4} = 8^{11}$.

    c Find the value of r when $4^r = \dfrac{1}{64}$.

    d Find the value of s when $512^{-\frac{2}{3}} = 2^s$.

    e Find the value of t when $125 = (25)^{2t-1}$.

12 A solid metal cylinder is of height 15 cm (to the nearest cm) and diameter 8.7 cm (to the nearest mm).

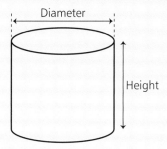

Diameter

Height

    a Copy and complete the following statements:

        i _____ ⩽ height < _____   Give your answers correct to 1 decimal place.

       ii _____ ⩽ radius < _____   Give your answers correct to 3 decimal places.

    b The density of a metal, in g/cm^3 is found from the formula

$$\text{Density} = \frac{\text{mass in g}}{\text{volume in cm}^3}$$

    The density of the metal is 7.8 g/cm^3, correct to 1 decimal place.

    Find the maximum and the minimum mass of the cylinder, correct to the nearest g/cm^3 (take $\pi = 3.14$).

    c Now use 3.142 for π.

    Find the percentage increase in the maximum mass of the cylinder. Give your answer correct to the nearest hundredth of a percent.

13 Simplify:

    a $\sqrt{72}$ **b** $\sqrt{10}(\sqrt{2} + \sqrt{10})$ **c** $\dfrac{2\sqrt{2} + 2\sqrt{3}}{\sqrt{6}}$

14 **a** Write 60 as the product of its prime factors. Write your answer in index form.

    b Find:

        i the highest common factor

       ii the lowest common multiple

    of 60 and 28.

15 A rectangle measures 8.4 cm long and 3.7 cm wide, both correct to the nearest mm.

    Find:

    a the smallest possible perimeter of the rectangle

    b the greatest possible area of the rectangle.

11 Probability

Learning outcomes

After this chapter you should be able to:

- calculate the probability of a single event as a fraction or a decimal
- understand relative frequency
- calculate the probability of simple combined events, using possibility diagrams and tree diagrams.

Revise 11.1 Probability

Equally likely outcomes

Probability is a measure of the likelihood of an **event** happening.

Something that is **impossible** has a probability of 0.

Something that is **certain** has a probability of 1.

All other probabilities lie between 0 and 1.

When two or more events have the same probability, they are called **equally likely outcomes.**

A coin is just as likely to land on heads as on tails.

A dice is just as likely to land on a 1, or a 2, or a 3, or a 4, or a 5, or a 6.

These are equally likely outcomes.

When all outcomes are equally likely,

$$\text{probability of an event} = \frac{\text{number of outcomes for the event}}{\text{total number of possible outcomes}}$$

A short way of writing 'The probability of a fair spinner landing on 4' is P(4).

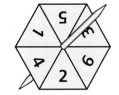

$P(4) = \frac{1}{6}$ ← The number of successful outcomes is 1 and the total number of possible outcomes is 6.

To find the probability of an outcome *not* happening, use the formula:

probability of an outcome not happening = 1 − probability of the outcome happening

So, P(not 4) = $1 - \frac{1}{6} = \frac{5}{6}$

Rolling a fair dice is an example of a **random** event.

Random means there is no reason why any outcome is more likely than any other.

Exam tip

You can write probabilities as fractions, decimals or percentages. Do not write probabilities as ratios.

Experimental probability

Probability can also be found by repeating an experiment. This is useful in industry for quality control, where a sample of items can be tested for faults.

You can use experimental data by repeating an experiment a large number of times.

These experiments are called **trials**.

The **relative frequency** is defined by the formula:

$$\text{relative frequency} = \frac{\text{number of outcomes for the event}}{\text{total number of trials}}$$

As the number of trials increases, the relative frequency gets closer and closer to the **experimental probability**. For a large number of trials, the relative frequency can be thought of as the probability.

To find the experimental probabilities of some events, you have to rely on historical data. You do this by looking at the frequencies of similar events in the past, such as particular weather conditions or patterns in the behaviour of a volcano.

Combined events

Sample space diagrams

A **sample space diagram** is a list or table of all possible outcomes.

Sample space diagrams are very useful when studying two events.

The addition rule

When more than one outcome is a successful outcome, the individual probabilities are added.

For example, the probability of a dice landing on an even number is $\frac{3}{6}$, and the probability of it landing on a 5 is $\frac{1}{6}$.

The probability of it landing on *either* an even number *or* a 5 is:

$$P(\text{even}) + P(5) = \frac{3}{6} + \frac{1}{6} = \frac{4}{6} = \frac{2}{3}$$

This is only true for **mutually exclusive** events.

Mutually exclusive events are events which cannot occur together.

> **Exam tip**
>
> The addition rule is the OR rule, when one thing OR another is required.

Rolling an odd number on a dice or rolling a 2 are mutually exclusive events.

Winning a race or coming third are mutually exclusive events.

But winning a race or finishing in the first three are not mutually exclusive events, because if you win you also finish in the first three.

For example, rolling an even number or a multiple of 3 are *not* mutually exclusive events.

This is because 6 is an even number *and* is a multiple of 3, so it can belong with either event.

The multiplication rule

To find the probability of two events both happening, the individual probabilities are multiplied.

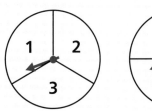

The two-way table shows you that the probability of both spinners landing on 2 is $\frac{1}{12}$.

These are **independent events** as the outcome of the first spinner does not affect the outcome of the second spinner.

		Four-part spinner			
		1	2	3	4
Three-part spinner	1				
	2				
	3				

Exam tip

The multiplication rule is the AND rule, when one thing AND another are both required.

P(both 2) = P(three-part spinner is 2) $\times$ P(four-part spinner is 2)

$$= \frac{1}{3} \times \frac{1}{4} = \frac{1}{12}$$

A bag contains 5 red counters and 3 blue counters.

Alice chooses one without looking, so the choice is random.

She notes the colour and then puts it back.

Megan then chooses a counter at random.

These are independent events.

But if Alice did not replace her counter, then the events would not be independent.

If Alice chose a red counter, the probability of Megan choosing a blue counter is $\frac{3}{7}$ as there are 3 blue counters and 4 red counters left.

But if Alice chose a blue counter, the probability of Megan choosing a blue counter is $\frac{2}{7}$ as there are 2 blue counters and 5 red counters left.

This is called **conditional probability** as the probabilities for Megan's choice depend on Alice's choice.

Suppose a class contains 6 boys and 4 girls. The teacher selects at random two students to represent the class.

The probability that the teacher selects two students of the same gender =

P(boy first) $\times$ P (boy second) $+$ P(girl first) $\times$ P (girl second)

$$= \frac{6}{10} \quad \times \quad \frac{5}{9} \quad + \quad \frac{4}{10} \quad \times \quad \frac{3}{9}$$

$$= \quad \frac{1}{3} \quad + \quad \frac{2}{15}$$

$$= \frac{5}{12} + \frac{2}{15} = \frac{7}{15}$$

Probability tree diagrams

When all the outcomes are not equally likely, a probability **tree diagram** can be used.

A probability tree diagram shows all the outcomes for each event, and the probabilities.

Separate sets of branches are used for each event.

The probabilities are written on each branch.

Worked examples

Equally likely outcomes

A bag contains tiles that spell the word:

        E

A tile is chosen at random.

a What is the probability that it has on it:

   i the letter E   **ii** a letter from the first half of the alphabet?

b What is:

   i P(not E)   **ii** P(a letter from the second half of the alphabet)?

Solution

a **i** There are 9 tiles, and 3 show the letter E.

So, $P(E) = \dfrac{\text{number of ways of chosing a letter E}}{\text{total number of tiles}} = \dfrac{3}{9} = \dfrac{1}{3}$

  ii The letters from the first half of the alphabet are E, L, E, H, E.

So P(a letter from the first half of the alphabet) $= \dfrac{5}{9}$

b **i** $P(\text{not E}) = 1 - P(E) = 1 - \dfrac{1}{3} = \dfrac{2}{3}$

  ii P(a letter from the second half of the alphabet)

$= 1 - P(\text{a letter from the first half of the alphabet})$

$= 1 - \dfrac{5}{9} = \dfrac{4}{9}$

Experimental probability

A company makes batteries.

They test a sample to see how long they last.

The results are shown in the table below:

Battery life, h (hours)	$0 < h \leqslant 20$	$20 < h \leqslant 40$	$40 < h \leqslant 60$	$60 < h \leqslant 80$	$80 < h \leqslant 100$	$100 < h \leqslant 120$
Frequency	7	27	51	129	75	11

a What is the experimental probability of a battery lasting more than 80 hours but no more than 100 hours?

b What is the experimental probability of a battery lasting more than 60 hours?

c The company makes 35 000 batteries in a week. How many would you expect to last more than 80 hours?

Solution

a They tested $7 + 27 + 51 + 129 + 75 + 11 = 300$ batteries.

75 lasted 80 hours but no more than 100 hours,

so the experimental probability is $\frac{75}{300} = \frac{1}{4}$ ◄────

> Cancelling by 75 makes the fraction simpler and easier to understand.

b $129 + 75 + 11 = 215$ lasted more than 60 hours.

The experimental probability is $\frac{215}{300} = \frac{43}{60}$ ◄────

> Cancelling by 5

c 86 lasted more than 80 hours, so you might expect $\frac{86}{300}$ of 35 000 to last more than 80 hours, or 10 033 to the nearest whole number.

Using a sample space diagram

Marcus is playing a game with two fair dice.

One is numbered 1, 2, 3, 4, 5 and 5.

The other is numbered 1, 2, 3, 4, 4, 4.

Marcus rolls each dice and adds the scores on the two dice together.

a Draw a sample space diagram to show this information.

b Use the sample space diagram to find:

  i the probability that the total score of the two dice is even

  ii the most likely total score, and the probability of that total score.

Solution

a

		First dice					
		1	**2**	**3**	**4**	**5**	**5**
Second dice	**1**	2	3	4	5	6	6
	2	3	4	5	6	7	7
	3	4	5	6	7	8	8
	4	5	6	7	8	9	9
	4	5	6	7	8	9	9
	4	5	6	7	8	9	9

b **i** 16 out of 36 outcomes are even, so P(even) $= \frac{16}{36} = \frac{4}{9}$.

  ii The most common score is 6, with a probability of $\frac{7}{36}$.

Probability tree diagram

A bag contains 5 blue discs and 3 red discs.

Nadira chooses a disc at random. She notes the colour and then replaces it.

Khalid then chooses a disc at random.

a **i** Show this information on a probability tree diagram.

  ii Calculate the probability that both discs chosen are the same colour.

b If instead of replacing it, Nadira keeps her disc. Now calculate the probability that both discs are the same colour.

Solution

a i

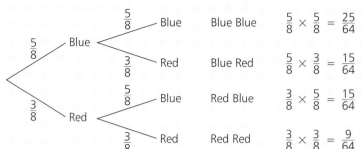

Nadira	Khalid	Outcome	Probability

$\frac{5}{8}$ Blue — Blue — Blue Blue — $\frac{5}{8} \times \frac{5}{8} = \frac{25}{64}$

> Multiply the probabilities as both events must happen.

$\frac{3}{8}$ Red — Blue Red — $\frac{5}{8} \times \frac{3}{8} = \frac{15}{64}$

$\frac{3}{8}$ Red — $\frac{5}{8}$ Blue — Red Blue — $\frac{3}{8} \times \frac{5}{8} = \frac{15}{64}$

$\frac{3}{8}$ Red — Red Red — $\frac{3}{8} \times \frac{3}{8} = \frac{9}{64}$

> On each set of branches, the probabilities will always add up to 1.

ii P(both the same colour) = P(both blue) + P(both red)

$$= \frac{25}{64} + \frac{9}{64}$$

$$= \frac{34}{64} = \frac{17}{32}$$

> Cancel by 2 to give the answer in its simplest form.

> Add the probabilities because one OR the other outcome is required.

b Khalid's probabilities depend on the colour of Nadira's disc:

If Nadira chooses a blue disc, there are 4 blue discs and 3 red discs for Khalid to choose from. But if Nadira chooses a red disc, Khalid chooses from 5 blue discs and 2 red discs.

Nadira	Khalid	Outcome	Probability

$\frac{5}{8}$ Blue — $\frac{4}{7}$ Blue — Blue Blue — $\frac{5}{8} \times \frac{4}{7} = \frac{20}{56} = \frac{5}{14}$

$\frac{3}{7}$ Red — Blue Red — $\frac{5}{8} \times \frac{3}{7} = \frac{15}{56}$

$\frac{3}{8}$ Red — $\frac{5}{7}$ Blue — Red Blue — $\frac{3}{8} \times \frac{5}{7} = \frac{15}{56}$

$\frac{2}{7}$ Red — Red Red — $\frac{3}{8} \times \frac{2}{7} = \frac{6}{56} = \frac{3}{28}$

P(both the same colour) = P(both blue) + P(both red)

$$= \frac{5}{14} + \frac{3}{28}$$

$$= \frac{10}{28} + \frac{3}{28} = \frac{13}{28}$$

Practise 11.1

1 A bag of fruit contains 6 apples, 3 bananas, 1 pear and 2 oranges.

Augusta takes at random one piece of fruit.

What is the probability that she gets:

a a banana

b a mango?

2 A bag contains some discs.

12 discs are red, 8 discs are blue and 5 discs are yellow.

A disc is chosen at random.

Find, as a fraction, the probability of each of the following events:

a The disc is red.

b The disc is red or yellow.

c The disc is not yellow.

3 A bag contains some red counters, some blue counters and some green counters.

The probability of choosing at random a red counter is $\frac{2}{11}$.

The probability of choosing at random a blue counter is $\frac{5}{11}$.

a Find the probability of choosing a green counter.

b There are 8 red counters in the bag.

How many counters are there altogether?

4 Richard has a bag of 30 keys.

Some unlock only his front door, some unlock only his back door, some unlock both and some unlock neither.

The numbers are indicated in the table below.

	Front door only	Back door only	Both doors	Neither
Number of keys	6	12	9	

a How many keys unlock neither door?

b What is the probability that a key selected at random from the bag will unlock both doors?

c What is the probability that a key selected at random will unlock his front door?

d Richard selects at random a key from the bag. It unlocks his front door. What is the probability that it will unlock his back door?

5 A ball is rolled down a slope with nails.

The ball eventually falls into one of five boxes, labelled A, B, C, D or E.

Sadiq rolls the ball 50 times.

The table shows his results:

Box	A	B	C	D	E
Frequency	6	10	15	13	6

Mouna rolls the ball 200 times. Here are her results:

Box	A	B	C	D	E
Frequency	15	51	72	49	13

The ball is rolled down the slope again.

a Use Sadiq's results to calculate an estimate for the probability that the ball falls:

  i into box A **ii** into box C **iii** not into box C.

b Use Mouna's results to calculate an estimate for the probability that the ball falls:

  i into box A **ii** into box C **iii** not into box C.

c Whose results do you think give more accurate probabilities? Give a reason for your answer.

d What could be done to get a better estimate for these probabilities?

6 A factory tests a sample of switches.

The switches are switched on and off repeatedly until they break.

The results are shown below.

Number of times switched, n	Number that broke
$0 \leqslant n < 500$	11
$500 \leqslant n < 1000$	4
$1000 \leqslant n < 1500$	5
$1500 \leqslant n < 2000$	7
$2000 \leqslant n < 2500$	9
$2500 \leqslant n < 3000$	11
$3000 \leqslant n < 3500$	14
$3500 \leqslant n < 4000$	17
$n \geqslant 4000$	22

a Calculate the probability that a switch will break after 3000 uses but before 3501 uses.

b If the company make 6000 switches in a week, how many are likely to break in under 1000 uses?

7 There are 15 counters, all the same size, in a bag.

Seven are blue, five are white and the rest are red.

Melissa takes a counter without looking, records its colour and replaces it in the bag. She then does this a second time.

Find the probability that:

a the first counter taken is red

b the first counter taken is red or white

c both counters are white.

8 When Luella goes to work, she either goes by car or cycles.

The probability that she goes by car is $\frac{3}{5}$.

At lunchtime she either goes to the canteen or the gym.

The probability that she goes to the canteen is $\frac{4}{5}$.

a Draw a probability tree diagram to show her possible choices.

b Find the probability that:

   i she cycles and goes to the canteen

   ii she cycles or goes to the gym or does both.

9 The probability that Mike is late for school on any day is $\frac{1}{8}$.

a Complete the probability tree diagram for Monday and Tuesday.

Monday　　　　　　　**Tuesday**

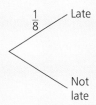

$\frac{1}{8}$　Late

Not late

b Calculate the probability that Mike is late on at least one of these days.

10 Kirsty has three discs.

Each disc has a different number on each side.

The table below shows the numbers on each disc.

	Disc 1	Disc 2	Disc 3
Side A	3	5	6
Side B	6	8	7

Kirsty flips the three discs and adds together the three numbers that face upwards.

a Calculate the probability that the Kirsty's total is greater than 16.

b Kirsty wants to flip two of the discs to obtain a total of 11.

Calculate the probability of Kirsty getting a total of 11 from:

   i disc 1 and disc 2

   ii disc 1 and disc 3

   iii disc 2 and disc 3

   iv two discs selected at random.

12 Further algebra

Learning outcomes

After this chapter you should be able to:

- transform more complicated formulae
- solve simultaneous linear equations in two unknowns
- solve simple linear inequalities and represent them on a graph
- multiply two brackets
- factorise expressions as the product of two brackets
- simplify algebraic fractions
- solve quadratic equations by factorisation
- solve quadratic equations by using the formula
- solve simultaneous equations when one is quadratic

Revise 12.1 Formulae and simultaneous equations

Transforming more complicated formulae

Changing the subject of a formula is similar to solving an equation.

The new subject must appear on the left-hand side.

Work towards this, one step at a time.

If the new subject letter appears on both sides of the formula, first collect terms containing that letter on one side of the formula, as shown in the second worked example.

Simultaneous equations

There are two methods for solving **simultaneous equations**: elimination and substitution.

Solving by elimination

You need matching coefficients in order to eliminate one of the variables.

For example, if you add these equations:
$$7x + 2y = 3$$
$$3x - 2y = 7$$

you eliminate y, and have the equation: $\quad 10x = 10$

which tells you that: $\quad x = 1$

> The rule is:
>
> **Signs Same Subtract**
>
> **Signs Different Add**

Substitute this value for x in the first equation:

$$7 + 2y = 3$$
$$2y = -4$$
$$y = -2$$

You may have to multiply one or both of the equations to get matching coefficients, as shown in the worked example.

Solving by substitution

Rearrange one of the equations to make x or y the subject.

Then substitute the expression for this variable in the second equation.

For example, given these equations:

$$x + 3y = 5$$

$$3x + 8y = 12$$

make x the subject of the first equation: $\qquad x = 5 - 3y$

and substitute this in the second equation: $\quad 3(5 - 3y) + 8y = 12$

$$15 - 9y + 8y = 12$$

$$15 - y = 12$$

$$y = 3$$

Exam tip

Don't forget to find the values of both the unknowns when you solve a pair of simultaneous equations.

Substitute this value for y in the expression for x:

$$x = 5 - 9 = -4$$

The solution is: $\quad x = -4, y = 3$.

Substitution is a useful method if one of the equations is in the form $x = ...$ or $y = ...$, as that equation is ready to be substituted.

It is also a quick method if one of the equations has an unknown with a coefficient of 1, such as $3x + y = 7$, or $x - 4y = 2$, as it can be instantly rearranged into the form $x = ...$ or $y = ...$ without dividing.

If both equations are of the form $ax + by = c$, then elimination is often simpler.

Worked examples

The radius of a sphere

The formula for the surface area of a sphere is $A = 4\pi r^2$, where r is the radius of the sphere.

Make r the subject of the formula.

Solution

Start by changing over the sides of the equation to get r on the left-hand side:

$$4\pi r^2 = A$$

Divide both sides by 4π to get r^2 on its own:

$$r^2 = \frac{A}{4\pi}$$

Take the square root of both sides:

$$r = \sqrt{\frac{A}{4\pi}}$$

Subject is on both sides of the equation

Make x the subject of: $4x - y = a(x - 5y)$.

Solution

Collect the terms that include x on one side of the formula:

$$4x - y = a(x - 5y)$$
$$4x - y = ax - 5ay \quad \longleftarrow \quad \boxed{\text{Multiply out the brackets.}}$$
$$4x - y + y = ax - 5ay + y \quad \longleftarrow \quad \boxed{\text{Add } y \text{ to both sides.}}$$
$$4x - ax = ax - 5ay + y - ax \quad \longleftarrow \quad \boxed{\text{Subtract } ax \text{ from both sides.}}$$
$$4x - ax = -5ay + y$$
$$x(4 - a) = y(1 - 5a) \quad \longleftarrow \quad \boxed{\text{Factorise both sides.}}$$
$$x = \frac{y(1 - 5a)}{(4 - a)} \quad \longleftarrow \quad \boxed{\text{Divide both sides by } (4 - a).}$$

Simultaneous equations

Solve the simultaneous equations:

$$2p - 3q = 13$$
$$5p - 2q = 16$$

Solution

There are no matching coefficients so you have to multiply the equations.

Multiply the first equation by 2 and the second equation by 3 to get $-6q$ in both equations:

$$4p - 6q = 26$$
$$15p - 6q = 48$$

Follow the rule 'Signs Same Subtract':

$$11p = 22 \quad \longleftarrow \quad \boxed{\text{Subtract first equation from second equation.}}$$
$$p = 2$$

Substitute $p = 2$ in the first equation:

$$4 - 3q = 13$$
$$-3q = 9$$
$$q = -3$$

Solution is: $p = 2, q = -3$. $\quad \longleftarrow \quad \boxed{\text{Check by substituting in the second equation:} \\ (5 \times 2) - (2 \times -3) = 10 - -6 = 16 \quad \checkmark}$

Revise 12.2 Inequalities

Inequalities

There are four **inequality** symbols:

$<$	$\leqslant$	$>$	$\geqslant$
Less than	Less than or equal to	Greater than	Greater than or equal to

To solve an inequality (or **inequation**), take the same steps as you would to solve an equation.

Equation: $3x - 7 = 17$ Inequality: $3x - 7 < 17$
$$3x = 24 \qquad\qquad\qquad 3x < 24$$
$$x = 8 \qquad\qquad\qquad\quad x < 8$$

There is one very important difference between solving an inequality and solving an equation.

If you multiply or divide both sides of an inequality by a negative number, the inequality is reversed.

$$4 < 5 \quad \text{but} \quad -4 > -5$$
so if $a < b$ then $-a > -b$

> **Exam tip**
> - Do *not* replace the inequality sign with an equals sign.
> - Make sure your answer includes the correct inequality sign.

A double inequality can be solved by splitting it into two separate inequalities:
$$2x - 5 \leqslant 3x - 1 < x + 9$$
can be split into $2x - 5 \leqslant 3x - 1$ and $3x - 1 < x + 9$
Solving $2x - 4 \leqslant 3x$ $3x < x + 10$
$$-4 \leqslant x \qquad\qquad\qquad 2x < 10$$
$$x < 5$$

The solution is $-4 \leqslant x < 5$
This can be shown on a number line:

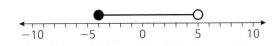

The filled circle shows that x can equal -4. The unfilled circle shows that x cannot equal 5.

Inequalities on a graph

You can represent an inequality, such as $x + y \geqslant 5$, as a **region** on a graph.
The **boundary** of this region will be the line $x + y = 5$.

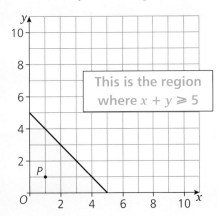

This is the region where $x + y \geqslant 5$

> **Exam tip**
> - You must show clearly which part of your graph is the required region.
> - It is a good idea to mark the region with the letter R.

The inequality $x + y \geqslant 5$ is called an included inequality because values include $x + y = 5$.
Which side of the boundary represents the inequality?
Pick a point such as (0, 0), (1, 0) or (0, 1) and check whether it satisfies the inequality.

For example, $P(1, 1)$ does *not* satisfy $x + y \geqslant 5$, so this point is *not* in the region.

Worked examples

Solving inequalities

Solve the inequality: $7 - 3x > 5(x + 3)$.

Solution

$$7 - 3x > 5x + 15$$

$$7 \quad > 8x + 15 \quad \longleftarrow \qquad \boxed{\text{Add } 3x \text{ to both sides.}}$$

$$-8 \quad > 8x \quad \longleftarrow \qquad \boxed{\text{Subtract 15 from both sides.}}$$

$$x < -1 \quad \longleftarrow \qquad \boxed{\text{Divide both sides by 8.}}$$

Using inequalities to define a region

Show the region bounded by these inequalities: $x > 2$, $y > 1$ and $x + 2y \leqslant 8$.

Solution

The line $x = 2$ is parallel to the y-axis, and $y = 1$ is parallel to the x-axis.

The line $x + 2y = 8$ can be drawn by finding two points. When $x = 0$, $2y = 8$, so $y = 4$. The line passes through $(0, 4)$.

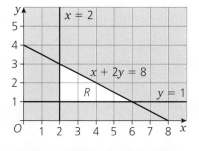

When $y = 0$, $x = 8$, so the line passes through $(8, 0)$.

Shade the regions which do not satisfy each inequality.

$x > 2$ is to the right of $x = 2$, so shade the region to the left.

$y > 1$ is above $y = 1$, so shade the region below.

$x + 2y \leqslant 8$ is below $x + 2y = 8$, so shade the region above.

The triangular region marked R is the region that satisfies all three inequalities.

Revise 12.3 Brackets, fractions and quadratic equations

Multiplying two brackets

Each term in one bracket has to be multiplied by each term in the other bracket.

Using a grid

Multiply out: $(2x - 5)(2x - 1)$.

×	2x	−5
2x	$4x^2$	$-10x$
−1	$-2x$	$+5$

$$(2x - 5)(2x - 1) = 4x^2 - 12x + 5$$

Using FOIL

Multiply out: $(y + 3)(3y - 2)$.

First terms: $(y + 3)(3y - 2)$ $y \times 3y = 3y^2$

Outer terms: $(y + 3)(3y - 2)$ $y \times -2 = -2y$

Inner terms: $(y + 3)(3y - 2)$ $+3 \times 3y = +9y$

Last terms: $(y + 3)(3y - 2)$ $+3 \times -2 = -6$

$$(y + 3)(3y - 2) = 3y^2 + 7y - 6$$

Separating out the first bracket

Multiply out: $(z - 4)(5z - 3)$.

$$(z - 4)(5z - 3) \rightarrow z(5z - 3) - 4(5z - 3)$$
$$= 5z^2 - 3z - 20z + 12$$
$$= 5z^2 - 23z + 12$$

> **Exam tip**
>
> Remember that each sign belongs to the term that follows it.

Some useful results are:

$(x + a)^2 = (x + a)(x + a) = x^2 + ax + ax + a^2 = x^2 + 2ax + a^2$

$(x - a)^2 = (x - a)(x - a) = x^2 - ax - ax + a^2 = x^2 - 2ax + a^2$

$(x + a)(x - a) = x^2 - ax + ax - a^2 = x^2 - a^2$

So $(x + 4)^2 = x^2 + 8x + 16$ $(x - 3)^2 = x^2 - 6x + 9$ $(x + 5)(x - 5) = x^2 - 25$

Factorising quadratic expressions

This process is the opposite of multiplying out two brackets.

$$x^2 + 3x - 40 = (\ ?\ )(\ ?\ )$$

Using the **F** of FOIL, the first terms must be x and x.

Using the **L** of FOIL, the last terms must multiply together to give -40.

Possible factors of -40 are:

-1 and $+40$, $+1$ and -40,

-2 and $+20$, $+2$ and -20,

-4 and $+10$, $+4$ and -10,

-5 and $+8$, $+5$ and -8.

The Inner and Outer terms have to combine to get $+3x$.
The only factors that combine to give $+3$ are -5 and $+8$.

The solution is: $x^2 + 3x - 40 = (x - 5)(x + 8)$

> **Exam tip**
>
> - The brackets should always contain integers, not fractions or decimals.
> - Check your answer by multiplying out the brackets to see if you get the original quadratic expression.

The difference of two squares

The factors of $p^2 - q^2$ are $(p - q)(p + q)$.

For example: $x^2 - 49 = (x - 7)(x + 7)$

$25 - 4y^2 = (5 - 2y)(5 + 2y)$

Harder quadratics

When the coefficient of x^2 is not 1, there are more possible factors to consider.

For example:
$$3x^2 - x - 14 = (3x \dots)(x \dots)$$

The last terms in the brackets must multiply to -14.

Possible factors of -14 are:
$$-1 \text{ and } +14, +1 \text{ and } -14,$$
$$-2 \text{ and } +7, +2 \text{ and } -7.$$

You have to decide which factor of -14 goes in the bracket with $3x$ and which goes with x to give the middle term of $-x$.

The solution is:
$$3x^2 - x - 14 = (3x - 7)(x + 2)$$

Four-term expressions

To factorise a four-term expression, look at the terms in pairs to find a common factor.

For example:
$$x^2 - 5x - xy + 5y$$

can be split into $x^2 - 5x$, which factorises to $x(x - 5)$

and $-xy + 5y$, which factorises to $-y(x - 5)$.

So $x^2 - 5x - xy + 5y = x(x - 5) - y(x - 5)$
$$= (x - y)(x - 5)$$

You may have to rearrange the terms before you can find the common factors.

> It also factorises to $y(-x + 5)$, but the aim is to make the two factors in brackets the same.

> **Exam tip**
> - Find a factor for one pair of terms.
> - You should then expect to find the same factor in the other pair.

Algebraic fractions

Addition and subtraction

Use common denominators for addition and subtraction.

For example:
$$\frac{x}{3} + \frac{x}{4} = \frac{4x}{12} + \frac{3x}{12}$$
$$= \frac{7x}{12}$$

Dividing by a common factor

An algebraic fraction can be simplified by dividing the numerator and the denominator by a common factor.

For example:
$$\frac{4xy}{6y} = \frac{2x}{3}$$

> After dividing numerator and denominator by the common factor $2y$.

and $\dfrac{25 - y^2}{15 - 8y + y^2} = \dfrac{{}^1(5 - y)(5 + y)}{{}_1(5 - y)(3 - y)}$

$$= \frac{(5 + y)}{(3 - y)}$$

> **Exam tip**
> If you are told to simplify an algebraic fraction, you should expect to find a common factor.

Solving quadratic equations

By factorisation

If $a \times b = 0$, then either a or b (or both of them) must be 0.

To solve the quadratic equation $2x^2 + 5x - 7 = 0$, first factorise to get $(x - 1)(2x + 7) = 0$.

If $(x - 1)(2x + 7) = 0$, then either $(x - 1) = 0$ or $(2x + 7) = 0$

$(x - 1) = 0$ leads to $x = 1$, and $(2x + 7) = 0$ leads to $x = -3.5$

> Check your answer by substitution: $2 \times 1^2 + (5 \times 1) - 7 = 2 + 5 - 7 = 0$ ✓
>
> $2 \times (-3.5)^2 + (5 \times -3.5) - 7 = 24.5 - 17.5 - 7 = 0$ ✓

Some quadratics cannot be factorised. Instead you have to use other methods.

Using the formula

The formula $x = \dfrac{-b \pm \sqrt{b^2 - 4ac}}{2a}$ can be used to solve the

quadratic equation $ax^2 + bx + c = 0$.

> Make sure the quadratic equation is in this form before you start to write down values for a, b and c.

The second worked example shows how to use the formula.

> **Exam tip**
>
> - If you are told to give your answers correct to 1 or 2 decimal places, you have to use the formula.
> - If you are trying to find the square root of a negative number, go back and check your working. There is no square root of a negative number.

Solving quadratic inequalities

A quadratic inequality is solved in a similar way to a quadratic equation.

$x^2 - 2x - 3 > 0$ ←——————— First solve the equivalent equation.

$x^2 - 2x - 3 = 0$ ←——————— First, factorise if possible.

$(x - 3)(x + 1) = 0$

$x - 3 = 0$ or $x + 1 = 0$

$x = 3$ or $x = -1$

So $x^2 - 2x - 3 = 0$ when $x = 3$ or $x = -1$

Substitute values into $x^2 - 2x - 3$ to find when $x^2 - 2x - 3 > 0$

When $x = -2$, $x^2 - 2x - 3 = 4 + 4 - 3 = 5$ (positive)

When $x = 0$, $x^2 - 2x - 3 = 0 - 0 - 3 = -3$ (negative)

When $x = 4$, $x^2 - 2x - 3 = 16 - 8 - 3 = 5$ (positive)

So a number line showing values of $x^2 - 2x - 3$ looks like this:

```
 +  +  +  +  +  +  0  -  -  -  -  0  +  +  +  +  +
┼──┼──┼──┼──┼──┼──┼──┼──┼──┼──┼──┼──┼──┼──┼──┼──┼
-8 -7 -6 -5 -4 -3 -2 -1  0  1  2  3  4  5  6  7  8
```

So the solution is $x < -1$ or $x > 3$.

Solving simultaneous equations where one is quadratic

These are best solved by substitution.

To solve $x^2 + y^2 = 10$

and $\quad\quad 2x - y = 5$

make one of the unknowns the subject of the linear equation.

$2x - y = 5$ can be rearranged as $y = 2x - 5$

Substitute into the quadratic equation:

$x^2 + y^2 = 10$ becomes $x^2 + (2x - 5)^2 = 10$

Simplify: $x^2 + 4x^2 - 10x - 10x + 25 = 10$

$\quad\quad\quad\quad\quad\quad 5x^2 - 20x + 15 = 0$

Solve: $\quad\quad\quad\quad\quad x^2 - 4x + 3 = 0$ ◄———— Dividing by 5

$\quad\quad\quad\quad\quad\quad (x - 3)(x - 1) = 0$

$\quad\quad\quad\quad\quad\quad\quad x = 3 \text{ or } x = 1$

Substitute into the linear equation:

$2x - y = 5$		$2x - y = 5$
$x = 3:\quad 6 - y = 5$		$x = 1:\quad 2 - y = 5$
$x = 3, y = 1$	or	$x = 1, y = -3$

Points of intersection of graphs

A linear equation in two variables can be represented as a straight line on a graph.

Every point on the line has coordinates that satisfy its equation.

Here are the graphs of $y = 2x - 1$, shown in blue, and $x + y = 7$, in red.

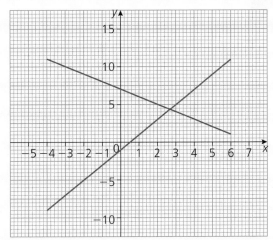

When you solve a pair of simultaneous equations, you are finding the values that fit both equations.

That is the point or points where the two graphs intersect.

Often, this is only an approximate solution, as the intersection may not fall exactly on the grid lines of the graph.

In this case, the point of intersection is approximately (2.7, 4.3).

So the approximate solution to the pair of equations is $x = 2.7, y = 4.3$

Here is the graph of $y = x^2$.

You can use it to solve equations such as $x^2 - 3x - 4 = 0$.

Rewrite $x^2 - 3x - 4 = 0$ in the form $x^2 = ...$
to match the right-hand side of $y = x^2$.

$x^2 = 3x + 4$.

The solutions are the x-coordinate points where
$y = x^2$ and $y = 3x + 4$ intersect.

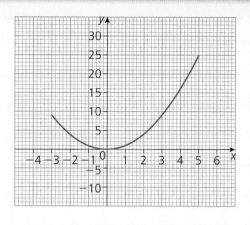

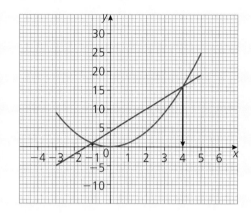

The solutions of $x^2 - 3x - 4$ are $x = -1$ and $x = 4$.

Worked examples

Algebraic fractions

Simplify: $\dfrac{3}{x - 2} - \dfrac{2}{x - 3}$

Solution

Put a bracket around each denominator:

$$\frac{3}{(x - 2)} - \frac{2}{(x - 3)}$$

The common denominator is $(x - 2)(x - 3)$:

$$\frac{3}{(x - 2)} - \frac{2}{(x - 3)} = \frac{3(x - 3)}{(x - 2)(x - 3)} - \frac{2(x - 2)}{(x - 2)(x - 3)}$$

$$= \frac{3x - 9 - 2x + 4}{(x - 2)(x - 3)} \longleftarrow \boxed{-2 \times -2 = +4}$$

$$= \frac{x - 5}{(x - 2)(x - 3)}$$

Solving a quadratic equation by the formula

Solve the equation: $3x^2 - 5x - 4 = 0$, giving your answers correct to 2 decimal places.

Solution

Start by writing down the values of a, b and c. ◄——— Make sure you include their signs.

$$a = 3, b = -5, c = -4$$

Substitute into the formula.

Start by working out the value of $b^2 - 4ac$ ◄——— Be very careful with the negative signs.

$$b^2 - 4ac = (-5)^2 - 4 \times 3 \times (-4)$$

$$= 25 + 48 = 73$$

$$x = \frac{--5 \pm \sqrt{73}}{2 \times 3}$$

$$= \frac{5 \pm 8.544...}{6}$$

$$= \frac{5 + 8.544...}{6} \quad \text{or} \quad \frac{5 - 8.544...}{6}$$

$$= \frac{13.544...}{6} \quad \text{or} \quad \frac{-3.544...}{6}$$

$$= 2.257... \quad \text{or} \quad -0.590...$$

Solution: $x = 2.26$ or -0.59 (to 2 d.p.)

Practise 12.1 – 12.3

1 Make r the subject of the formula $V = \pi r^2 h$.

2 Solve these inequalities:

   a $3x - 2 \geqslant 16$

   b $y + 7 < 11 + 5y$

3 Find the coordinates of the point of intersection of the straight lines:

$$4x + y = 5$$
$$2x - 5y = 8$$

4 The region inside this quadrilateral is defined by four inequalities.

One of these is $x + y \geqslant -2$.

Write down the other three inequalities.

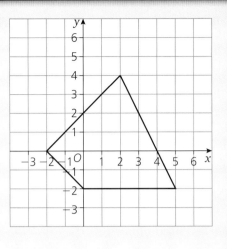

5 Here is the graph of $y = x^2 - 3$.

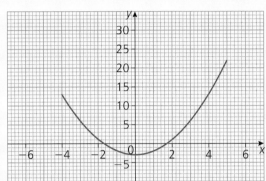

Find the equation of a line that should be drawn on the grid in order to solve the equation $x^2 - 3x = 5$.

6 Multiply out and simplify:

a $(p + 8)(p - 8)$

b $(4q - 3)(q + 2)$

7 Factorise:

a $m^2 + 8m + 7$

b $n^2 - n - 6$

c $5t^2 + 3t - 2$

d $pq - 2p - 10 + 5q$

8 Factorise completely:

a $3x^2 - 3$

b $2y^2 - 12y + 18$

[Hint: Take out a single term factor first, then factorise into two brackets.]

9 Simplify:

a $\dfrac{3}{2x} - \dfrac{2}{5x}$

b $\dfrac{y^2 - 5y + 4}{2y^2 - 7y - 4}$

10 a Solve the equation $2x^2 + 7x - 15 = 0$.

b Solve the equation $4m^2 + m - 1 = 0$, giving your solutions correct to 2 decimal places.

11 Solve the simultaneous equations:

$a^2 - 2b = 23$

$3a + b = 16$

12 Here are the graphs of $y = 2x^2 - 5$ and $y = 12 - 3x$.

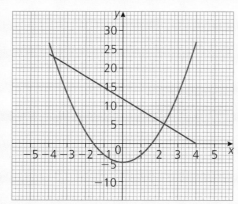

The x-coordinates of the points of intersection of the graphs are the solutions to an equation of the form $ax^2 + bx + c = 0$.

a Find the values of a, b and c.

b Solve the equation algebraically, showing full working. Give your answers to 1 decimal place.

13 Simplify:

a $\dfrac{3x}{2y} + \dfrac{x}{3y}$ **b** $\dfrac{5x}{2a} \div \dfrac{3xy}{2a^2}$ **c** $\dfrac{3x^2 - 6x}{x^2 - x - 2}$

14 The sum of Lynda's age and John's age now is 64.

a If Lynda is x years old, write down John's age in terms of x.

Six years ago, John's age was exactly double Linda's age.

b Use this information to write down an equation and solve it to find their ages now.
Show clear algebraic working.

13 Trigonometry

Learning outcomes

After this chapter you should be able to:

- apply Pythagoras' theorem
- apply the sine, cosine and tangent ratios for acute angles to the calculation of a side or an angle of a right-angled triangle
- interpret and use three-figure bearings measured clockwise from the North (i.e. 000°–360°)
- solve problems involving angles of elevation and depression
- extend sine and cosine values to angles between 90° and 180°, and use the sine and cosine rules for any triangle
- use the trigonometrical formula for the area of a triangle
- solve simple trigonometrical problems in three dimensions.

Revise 13.1 Trigonometry

Pythagoras' theorem

The longest side of a right-angled triangle is always opposite the right angle. It is called the **hypotenuse**.

If the shorter sides of a right-angled triangle are a and b, and the hypotenuse is c, then Pythagoras' theorem states that:

$a^2 + b^2 = c^2$

You can split rectangles and isosceles triangles into two right-angled triangles.

Exam tip

Pythagoras' theorem only works for right-angled triangles.

Length of a line segment

You can use Pythagoras' theorem to find the length of a line segment. The second worked example shows how to do this.

Trigonometry

Trigonometry is the study of the lengths of sides and sizes of angles in triangles.

A right-angled triangle has a hypotenuse.

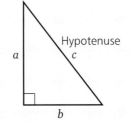

The two shorter sides are named according to their position.

In the diagram, the base is opposite to the angle $x°$, and so it is called the **opposite side**.

The third side is called the **adjacent side**, because it is adjacent to, or next to, the angle of $x°$.

The **sine** of $x° = \dfrac{\text{opposite side}}{\text{hypotenuse}}$

The **cosine** of $x° = \dfrac{\text{adjacent side}}{\text{hypotenuse}}$

The **tangent** of $x° = \dfrac{\text{opposite side}}{\text{adjacent side}}$

These are usually abbreviated to the first three letters, so you write:

$$\sin x = \frac{\text{opp}}{\text{hyp}} \qquad \cos x = \frac{\text{adj}}{\text{hyp}} \qquad \tan x = \frac{\text{opp}}{\text{adj}}$$

> **Exam tip**
>
> You must learn these three formulae.
>
> You can remember these by learning the word SOHCAHTOA.
>
> Or use a mnemonic such as 'Some Old Hairy Camels Are Hairier Than Others Are'.

The values of sine, cosine and tangent for any angle can be obtained from your calculator.

Pressing the keys [sin] [7] [2] [=] gives an answer of 0.95105651...

This is the sine of an angle of 72°.

Pressing the keys [inv] [cos] [0] [.] [6] [0] [1] [8] gives an answer of 53.0010...

This tells you that the angle of 53.0010° has a cosine of 0.6018

This can be written as: $\cos^{-1} 0.6018 = 53.0010...°$

> **Exam tip**
>
> To do these calculations your calculator must be in 'degree' mode. Check that a small 'd' or 'deg' is showing on the display.

Angles of elevation and depression

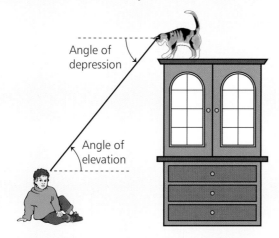

When you look up from the horizontal, you look through an **angle of elevation**.

If you look down, the angle between the horizontal and the line of sight is an **angle of depression**.

Bearings

Angle bearings are measured clockwise, from North.

Bearings are always written as 3-figure bearings.

If the angle is less than 100°, write a 0 before it.

So a bearing of 27° is written as 027°.

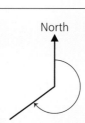

North

Worked examples

Height and area of an isosceles triangle

An isosceles triangle has two sides of 12 cm and one of 8 cm.

Calculate:

a the perpendicular height of the triangle

b the area of the triangle.

Solution

a Draw the perpendicular height which bisects the base of the triangle. Then use Pythagoras' theorem on one of the right-angled triangles.

In the right-hand triangle:

$$a^2 + b^2 = c^2$$

$$a^2 + 4^2 = 12^2$$

$$a^2 + 16 = 144$$

$$a^2 = 128$$

$$a = \sqrt{128} = 11.313708\ldots \text{ cm} = 11.3 \text{ cm (to 1 d.p.)}$$

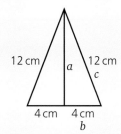

b Area $= \frac{1}{2} \times$ base $\times$ height $= \frac{1}{2} \times 8 \times 11.313708\ldots = 45.3 \text{ cm}^2$ (to 1 d.p.)

Exam tip

Avoid rounding until the end of the calculation.

Finding the length of a line segment

$A(4, -1)$ and $B(-2, -3)$ are the endpoints of a line segment.

Find the length of AB.

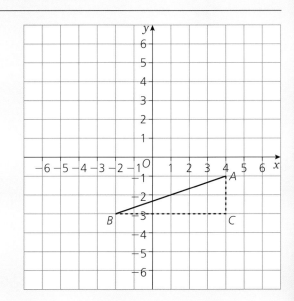

Solution

Draw in the triangle ABC.

AB is the hypotenuse of this triangle.

$$AB^2 = AC^2 + BC^2$$

$$= (-1 - -3)^2 + (4 - -2)^2$$

$$= 4 + 36 = 40$$

$$AB = \sqrt{40} = 2\sqrt{10} = 6.3 \text{ units (to 1 d.p.)}$$

Finding a length and angle of elevation

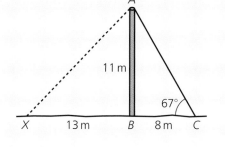

A vertical pole *AB* of length 11 m is held in place by a rope *AC* as shown.

C is 8 m from the foot of the pole.

The angle between the ground and the rope is 67°.

A point *X* is 13 m from the foot of the pole.

Calculate:

a the length of the rope

b the angle of elevation of the top of the pole from *X*.

Solution

a First, label the sides of triangle *ABC* opp, adj and hyp on the diagram.

AC is the hypotenuse as it is opposite to the right angle.

AB is opposite to the angle of 67° and *BC* is adjacent to it.

You know the length of the opposite side and need to find the length of *AC*, the hypotenuse.

Sine contains the opposite side and the hypotenuse.

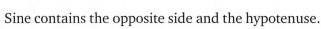

$$\sin 67° = \frac{\text{opp}}{\text{hyp}}$$

$$\sin 67° = \frac{11}{AC}$$

$$\sin 67° \times AC = 11$$

$$AC = \frac{11}{\sin 67°}$$

$$AC = 11.9 \text{ m (to 1 d.p.)}$$

b First, label the sides of triangle *AXB* opp, adj and hyp on the diagram.

AX is the hypotenuse as it is opposite to the right angle.

AB is opposite to the angle *AXB* and *BX* is adjacent to it.

Use tangent as you know the opposite and adjacent sides.

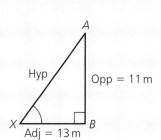

$$\tan AXB = \frac{\text{opp}}{\text{adj}}$$

$$\tan AXB = \frac{11}{13} = 0.84615\ldots$$

$$AXB = \tan^{-1} 0.84615\ldots$$

$$AXB = 40.2° \text{(to 1 d.p.)}$$

Finding a bearing

Three towns, A, B and C are situated so that B is 11 km due East of A, and C is 23 km due South of B.

Calculate the bearing of C from A.

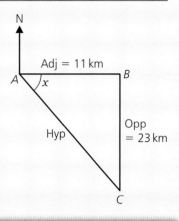

Solution

Draw a diagram.

You need to calculate angle x.

You know the opposite side and the adjacent side, so use the tangent:

$$\tan x = \frac{\text{opp}}{\text{adj}}$$

$$\tan x = \frac{23}{11} = 2.090909\ldots$$

$$x = \tan^{-1} 2.090909\ldots = 64.4° \text{ (to 1 d.p.)}$$

The bearing of C from A is angle $NAC = 90° + 64.4° = 154.4°$

Exam tip

- Always draw and label a diagram.
- Always write down the appropriate formula for sin, cos or tan.
- Make sure you know how to use your calculator to find an angle from the sin, cos or tan by using the $\sin^{-1}$, $\cos^{-1}$ or $\tan^{-1}$ keys.

Revise 13.2 Trigonometry rules

Angles greater than 90 degrees

This is the graph of $y = \sin x°$.

It shows that $\sin x° = \sin (180 - x)°$.

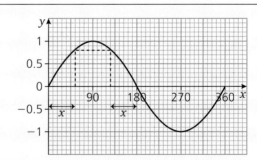

This is the graph of $y = \cos x°$.

It shows that $\cos x° = -\cos (180 - x)°$.

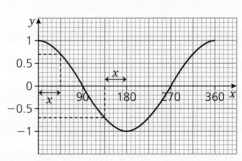

This is the graph of $y = \tan x°$

It shows that $\tan x° = -\tan(180 - x)°$.

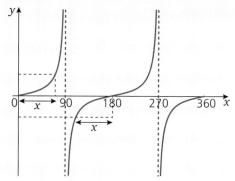

In triangle ABC, side a is opposite to angle A, side b is opposite to angle B and side c is opposite to angle C.

Then **sine rule** states that: $\dfrac{a}{\sin A} = \dfrac{b}{\sin B} = \dfrac{c}{\sin C}$

It can also be written as: $\dfrac{\sin A}{a} = \dfrac{\sin B}{b} = \dfrac{\sin C}{c}$

The **cosine rule** states that: $a^2 = b^2 + c^2 - 2bc \cos A$.

It can also be written as: $\qquad b^2 = a^2 + c^2 - 2ac \cos B$ (by replacing A with B, a with b and b with a)

or $\qquad\qquad\qquad\qquad c^2 = b^2 + a^2 - 2ba \cos C$ (by replacing A with C, a with c and c with a).

Using trigonometry, the area of a triangle can be calculated as:

$\qquad$ **Area** $= \frac{1}{2}ab \sin C$

It is also equal to $\frac{1}{2}ac \sin B$ and $\frac{1}{2}bc \sin A$.

Three dimensions

Trigonometry can be used in three dimensions.

You need to be able to identify right-angled triangles. See the second worked example.

Worked examples

Applying the sine rule and cosine rule

$ABCD$ is a quadrilateral.

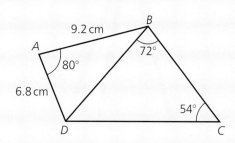

$AB = 9.2$ cm, $AD = 6.8$ cm, angle $BAD = 80°$, angle $BCD = 54°$ and angle $DBC = 72°$.

Calculate: $\quad$ **a** BD $\qquad\qquad$ **b** CD.

Solution

a In triangle *ABD,* you know the length of two sides and need to calculate the third length. You know the size of one angle.

The cosine rule contains three sides and one angle.

You know angle *A,* so use

$$a^2 = b^2 + c^2 - 2bc \cos A$$

As the vertices are *A, B* and *D,* you replace *c* with *d*:

$$a^2 = b^2 + d^2 - 2bd \cos A$$

$$a^2 = 6.8^2 + 9.2^2 - 2 \times 6.8 \times 9.2 \times \cos 80°$$

$$a^2 = 46.24 + 84.64 - 21.72685999...$$

$$a = \sqrt{109.15314...} = 10.4 \text{ cm (to 1 d.p.)}$$

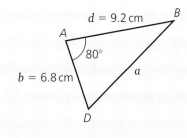

b In triangle *BCD,* you know two angles and the length of one side. You need to calculate another length.

The sine rule uses two angles and two lengths.

The angles are *B* and *C* and the sides are *b* and *c*.

To find a side, write the formula with the sides on top:

$$\frac{b}{\sin B} = \frac{c}{\sin C}$$

$$\frac{b}{\sin 72°} = \frac{10.4}{\sin 54°}$$

$$\frac{b}{\sin 72°} = 12.85510696...$$

$$b = 12.85510696... \times \sin 72° = 12.2 \text{ cm (to 1 d.p.)}$$

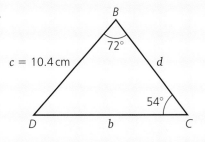

Finding the height of a 3-D object

A tripod has three legs *AB, AC* and *AD* of length 1.9 m.

The feet form an equilateral triangle *BCD* with sides of 0.7 m.

Calculate *AX,* the height of the tripod.

Solution

Draw a sketch of the equilateral triangle *BCD*.

BXC is an isosceles triangle. *XM* is the perpendicular bisector of *BC*.

In triangle *BXM*,

$$\cos 30° = \frac{BM}{BX}$$

$$BX = \frac{BM}{\cos 30°} = \frac{0.35}{0.866...} = 0.404 \text{ m (to the nearest mm)}$$

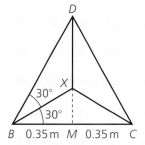

Draw triangle *ABX*.

Using Pythagoras' theorem:

$$BX^2 + AX^2 = AB^2$$

$$AX^2 = 1.9^2 - 0.404^2$$

$$AX^2 = 3.446784$$

$$AX = \sqrt{3.446784} = 1.86 \text{ m (to the nearest cm)}$$

Practise 13.1 – 13.2

1 An isosceles triangle *ABC* has *AB* = *AC* = 11 cm and *BC* = 9 cm.

Calculate the size of angle *ABC*.

2 The quadrilateral *ABCD* has *AB* = 9.7 cm,
CD = 3.2 cm, *AD* = 20 cm,
angle *BAD* = 67° and angle *ADC* = 90°.

Calculate the size of angle *BCD*.

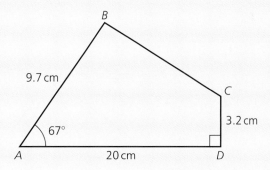

3 The diagram shows a ramp.

CD = 6 m and *BC* = 4.5 m

Angle *BED* = 35°

BE is a diagonal stripe painted on the ramp.

Calculate the size of:

a angle *BDC*   **b**   the length of *DE*.

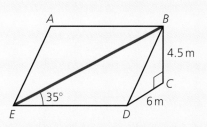

4 In triangle ABC, $AB = 8.6$ cm, $AC = 9.7$ cm
and angle $BAC = 61°$.

Calculate:

a the length of BC

b the size of angle ABC.

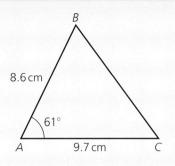

5 B is 9.2 km from A on a bearing of 058°.
C is 14.3 km from B.
The bearing of C from B is 160°.

Calculate:

a the size of angle ABC

b the distance from A to C

c the bearing of C from A.

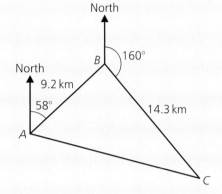

6 A tetrahedron has four faces that are all equilateral triangles.
The sides are all 12 cm.

a Calculate the surface area of the tetrahedron.

b If M is the midpoint of CD, calculate:

  i the length of BM

  ii the angle ABM.

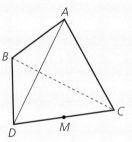

7 The diagram shows a tent.

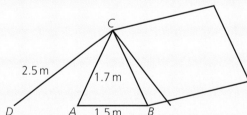

The front of the tent, ABC, is vertical and in the shape of an isosceles triangle.

$AC = BC = 1.7$ m, and $AB = 1.5$ m.

CD is a guy rope of length 2.5 m, attached to the top of the tent at C and pegged into the ground at D.

Calculate the angle between the guy rope and the ground.

14 Calculus

Learning outcomes

After this chapter you should be able to:

- understand the concept of a variable rate of change
- differentiate integer powers of x
- determine gradients and turning points by differentiation
- distinguish between maxima and minima by considering the shape of the graph
- apply calculus to linear kinematics.

Revise 14.1 Rates of change

When you turn on the taps to fill a bath, the water level in the bath changes.

The width of the bath is greater at the top than at the bottom.

This means that although the water level is always rising, the rate at which it rises is constantly decreasing.

The graph showing the water level over the time it is being filled might look like this:

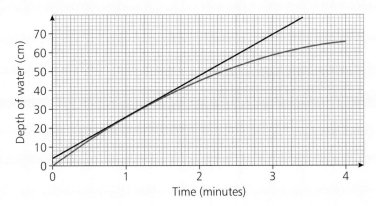

During the first minute, the water level has risen by nearly 26 cm. In the second minute, it rises another 20 cm.

The rate of change at any moment is equal to the gradient of the curve at that point.

The gradient of the curve is equal to the gradient of the tangent at that point.

The tangent, shown in black, passes through (0, 4) and (2, 48).

So the gradient $= \dfrac{48 - 4}{2 - 0} = 22$.

So at a time of 1 minute, the bath is filling at the rate of 22 cm/minute.

Worked examples

Gradient of a non-linear graph

The graph shows $y = f(x)$.

Find:

a $f(2)$

b the gradient of the graph when $x = 2$.

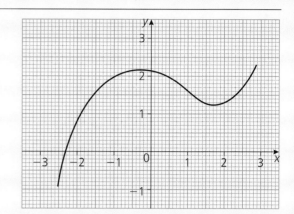

Solution

a $f(2)$ is the value of the function when $x = 2$.
The blue line shows that $f(2) = 1.3$

b To find the gradient when $x = 2$,
draw the tangent at $x = 2$, shown in red.

This passes through $(0, 0.4)$ and $(3, 1.75)$.

The gradient is $\dfrac{1.75 - 0.4}{3 - 0} = \dfrac{1.35}{3} = 0.45$

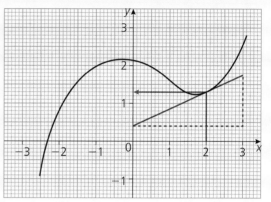

Revise 14.2 Differentiation

Differentiation is an algebraic method of finding rates of change.

Differentiating gives an expression for the gradient of a curve, allowing you to work out the gradient at any point.

If $y = ax^n$, where a and n are constants, then the derivative is

$\dfrac{dy}{dx} = nax^{n-1}$, or multiply by the power and then subtract 1 from the power.

To differentiate an expression made up of sums and differences of terms, differentiate each term.

For example, if $A = 5x^3 - 4x + \dfrac{1}{x^2} + 6$,

first rewrite as

$A = 5x^3 - 4x + x^{-2} + 6$

$\dfrac{dA}{dx} = 3 \times 5x^2 - 1 \times 4x^0 + (-2) \times x^{-3}$

$= 15x^2 - 4 - 2x^{-3}$

> Note: the constant term, 6, disappears when differentiated.

Maxima and minima

When the gradient of a graph changes, the gradient can change from positive to negative, or negative to positive. Such points are called **turning points**.

At a turning point the gradient is 0 as the tangent is parallel to the x-axis.

The **maximum** and **minimum** values of a function occur at turning points.

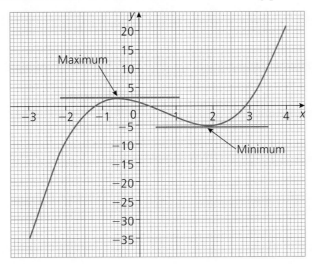

This is when the gradient $= 0$, or $\dfrac{\mathrm{d}y}{\mathrm{d}x} = 0$

Worked examples

Maxima and minima

A rectangle has a length of $5x$ cm and a width of $(3 - 2x)$ cm.
Find the maximum area of the rectangle.

Solution

The area, $A = 5x(3 - 2x)$
$\qquad = 15x - 10x^2$

The maximum and minimum values are found when the gradient is zero.

$\dfrac{\mathrm{d}A}{\mathrm{d}x} = 15 - 20x = 0$

$\qquad 15 = 20x$

$\qquad x = \dfrac{15}{20} = 0.75$

So the maximum area $= 5x(3 - 2x)$
$\qquad\qquad = (5 \times 0.75)(3 - 2 \times 0.75)$
$\qquad\qquad = 3.75 \times 1.5$
$\qquad\qquad = 5.625 \ \mathrm{cm}^2$

Revise 14.3 Kinematics

Kinematics is the study of moving objects.

When you cycle along the road, your speed is a measure of how quickly you are changing the distance you have travelled. Your velocity is your speed in a particular direction.

A speed of 4 m/s means that every second you move 4 m.

But your speed is rarely constant. If your speed is changing, then you would not necessarily travel 4 m every second. A speed of 4 m/s at a moment in time means that you would travel 4 m in a second if you maintained that speed.

So speed is the rate of change of distance travelled.

If your speed is changing then you can measure the rate of change. This is called acceleration (or deceleration if you are slowing down).

An acceleration of $2 \, \text{m/s}^2$ means that your speed is increasing by 2 m/s every second.

Gradient of a non-linear graph

The gradient of a graph shows the rate of change.

On a distance–time graph, the gradient shows the rate at which the distance is changing. This is the speed.

On a speed–time graph, the gradient shows the rate at which the speed is changing. This is the acceleration.

Speed and acceleration can also be found by differentiation.

If x is the distance travelled in a time t,

then the speed, $s = \dfrac{dx}{dt}$, because speed is the rate of change of distance.

Acceleration, $a, = \dfrac{ds}{dt}$ because acceleration is the rate of change of speed.

Worked examples

Kinematics

A ball is thrown vertically upwards.

Its height, h metres above the ground at time t seconds, is given by

$h = 15t - 5t^2 + 2$

a Find: **i** the height

           ii the velocity

           iii the acceleration of the ball at time 2 seconds.

b In which direction is the ball travelling at time 2 seconds?

Solution

a **i** $h = 15t - 5t^2 + 2$

$\qquad = 15 \times 2 - 5 \times 2^2 + 2$

$\qquad = 30 - 20 + 2 = 12\,\text{m}$

ii Velocity $v = \dfrac{\text{d}h}{\text{d}t} = 15 - 10t$

$\qquad\qquad\qquad = 15 - 10 \times 2$

$\qquad\qquad\qquad = 15 - 20 = -5\,\text{m/s}$

iii Acceleration $= \dfrac{\text{d}v}{\text{d}t} = -10\,\text{m/s}^2$

b As the velocity is negative, the ball is travelling downwards.

Practise 14.1 – 14.3

1 Use the graph to estimate the gradient of the curve when

  a $x = 0$

  b $x = 2$

  c $y = 2$

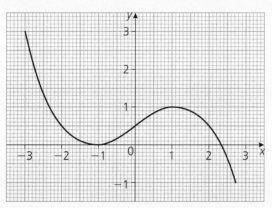

2 Match the distance–time graphs to the speed–time graphs that represent the same journeys.

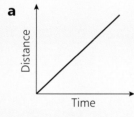

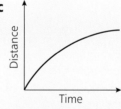

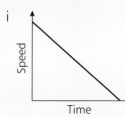
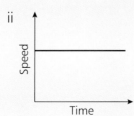
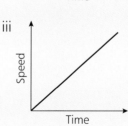

3 $y = 3x^2 - 5x$

Write down $\dfrac{\text{d}y}{\text{d}x}$

4 A scientist is growing bacteria in the laboratory.

During the first 10 days, the area of the bacteria, A mm^2, on day t, is given by

$A = t^2 - 0.5t + 1$

a Find $\dfrac{dA}{dt}$

b Find the rate of growth in mm^2/day on day 4.

5 $y = 2x^3 - \dfrac{1}{x^2} + 3$

a Find $\dfrac{dy}{dx}$

b Find the gradient of the graph of $y = 2x^3 - \dfrac{1}{x^2} + 3$ at the point where $x = 1$.

6 Find the coordinates of the turning point of $y = x^2 - 12x + 3$.

7 Find the minimum value of y when $y = 2x^2 - 4x - 3$.

8 A rocket is travelling so that its velocity, v m/s, at a time of t seconds after take-off, is given by the formula

$v = 6t^2 - 2t$

Calculate:

a its velocity at time 4 seconds

b its acceleration at time 4 seconds.

c the time it takes to reach an acceleration of 100 m/s^2 and its velocity at this moment.

9 A farmer has 40 m of fencing.

He uses the fencing to make 3 sides of a rectangular pen, using a long straight hedge as the fourth side.

The diagram shows the pen with an area of A m^2.

The width of the pen is x m.

The length of the pen is y m.

a Write y in terms of x.

b Show that $A = 40x - 2x^2$

c Find $\dfrac{dA}{dx}$

d Find the maximum value of A.

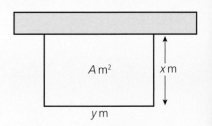

10 A car is travelling at a speed of 120 m/s.

Over the next 10 seconds the car maintains this speed for the first second, after which its speed, S m/s, after t seconds is given by

$$S = 150 - 10t - \frac{30}{t},$$

for $1 \leqslant t \leqslant 10$

Find the value of t when the car was travelling at its maximum speed, and the speed at that moment.

Practice exam questions: Paper 1

1    $A(-6, -4)$ and $B(3, -2)$ are 2 points.

Find the coordinates of the midpoint of AB.   *(2 marks)*

2   A square has side 5.7 cm correct to the nearest millimetre.

Calculate the lower bound of the area of the square.

Write down all the figures on your calculator.   *(2 marks)*

3   A bank pays compound interest at 4% per year.

Olaf invests $6000 for three years.

Calculate the interest earned over the three years.   *(3 marks)*

4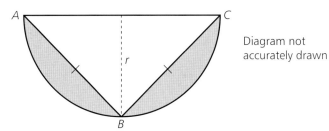

Diagram not accurately drawn

A triangle ABC is inside a semicircle, radius r. $AB = BC$.

Write down an expression, in its simplest form, for the shaded area.   *(4 marks)*

5   Evaluate $49^{\frac{1}{2}} \times 64^{\frac{2}{3}}$.   *(3 marks)*

6   Find the highest common factor of 324 and 504.   *(3 marks)*

7   Factorise $f^2 - 25g^2$.   *(2 marks)*

8   W is inversely proportional to the square of x.

When $x = 5$, $W = 10.2$.

Find the value of W when $x = 3$.   *(4 marks)*

9 Solve the equation

$$\frac{3}{x} + \frac{4}{x+2} = 1$$ *(5 marks)*

10 Solve the inequality $3(4x - 2) - 2(5x - 8) \leqslant 0$ *(3 marks)*

11 $(x + 3)(x - a) = x^2 - bx - 12$, for all values of x, where a and b are constants.

Find the values of a and b *(3 marks)*

12 The scale on a map is 1:50 000.

Find

a the actual distance apart, in km, of 2 places which are 3.5 cm apart on the map *(2 marks)*

b the actual area, in km², of a region that is 12.4 cm² on the map. *(4 marks)*

13 Work out $\dfrac{2.65 \times 10^{-3}}{4.78 \times 10^3}$.

Give your answer in standard form, correct to 2 significant figures. *(3 marks)*

14 Solve the simultaneous equations

$$\frac{3}{4}x - 2y = 12$$

$$6x + 11y = 15$$ *(4 marks)*

15 $\mathscr{E} = \{x: 0 < x < 20\}$

$P = \{x: x \text{ is a prime number}\}$

$M = \{x: x \text{ is a multiple of 4}\}$

$C = \{x: x \text{ is a factor of 24}\}$

a In the Venn diagram, write in the correct place

   i 8 *(1 mark)*

   ii 13. *(1 mark)*

b **i** List the elements of $P \cap M$ *(1 mark)*

   ii Write down the value of $n(P \cap C)$ *(2 marks)*

16

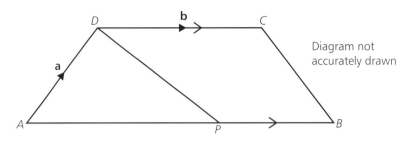

Diagram not accurately drawn

ABCD is a trapezium. $\overrightarrow{AD} = \mathbf{a}$, $\overrightarrow{DC} = \mathbf{b}$ and $AB = 2 \times DC$.

a Find, in terms of **a** and **b**

   i $\overrightarrow{AC}$ *(1 mark)*

   ii $\overrightarrow{CB}$. *(2 marks)*

b *P* is the point on *AB* such that $AP : PB = 3 : 2$.

   Find $\overrightarrow{DP}$ in terms of **a** and **b**. *(2 marks)*

17 $y = 2 + \dfrac{3}{x - 2}$

Rearrange the formula to make *x* the subject. *(4 marks)*

18   The shaded region is defined by 5 inequalities.

One of the inequalities is $y \geqslant -\frac{1}{2}x - 1$.

Find and write down the other 4 inequalities.

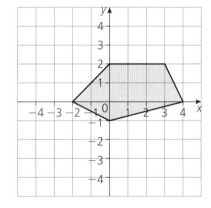

(5 marks)

19   The graph shows the journey of a metro train between two stations.

Calculate the acceleration, in m/s^2, during the first 40 seconds. *(1 mark)*

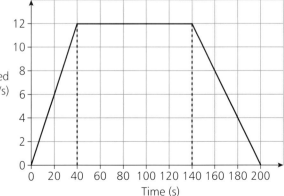

Speed (m/s)

Time (s)

20   *A, B, C* and *D* are points on the circumference of a circle, centre *O*.

DA = DC and angle *AOC* = 112°.

Calculate

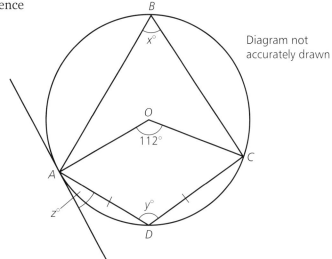

Diagram not accurately drawn

a   *x*   *(2 marks)*

b   *y*   *(2 marks)*

c   *z*   *(5 marks)*

giving your reasons in each case.

21   A bag contains 14 red balls and 11 blue balls.

A ball is taken at random from the bag and is not replaced.

Another ball is then taken at random from the bag.

a   If the first ball taken is red, explain why the probability that the second ball taken is also red is $\frac{13}{24}$.   *(1 mark)*

b

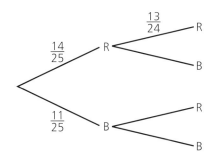

Copy and complete the probability tree diagram by writing the 3 remaining probabilities.   *(3 marks)*

c   Find the probability that at least one red ball is taken.   *(3 marks)*

Practice exam questions: Paper 2

1   A car dealer advertised a car for $8800.

    a   In a sale the price was reduced by 20%.

        Show that the cost in the sale was $7040. *(1 mark)*

    b   The advertised $8800 was 60% more than the dealer paid for the car.

        Calculate how much the dealer paid for the car. *(3 marks)*

2   The table shows the marks out of 100 gained by 80 students in a mathematics exam.

$0 < x \leqslant 10$	$10 < x \leqslant 20$	$20 < x \leqslant 30$	$30 < x \leqslant 40$	$40 < x \leqslant 50$
0	9	10	12	15

$50 < x \leqslant 60$	$60 < x \leqslant 70$	$70 < x \leqslant 80$	$80 < x \leqslant 90$	$90 < x \leqslant 100$
16	8	6	3	1

    a   Write down the modal class interval. *(1 mark)*

    b   Calculate an estimate of the mean. *(4 marks)*

    c   Make a cumulative frequency table for the data. *(2 marks)*

    d   Using a scale of 2 cm for 10 marks on the horizontal axis and 2 cm for 10 students on the vertical axis, draw the cumulative frequency graph. *(4 marks)*

    e   Use your cumulative frequency graph to find an estimate of

      i   the median *(1 mark)*

      ii   the interquartile range *(2 marks)*

      iii   the number of students gaining more than 65 marks. *(2 marks)*

3   The table shows some of the values of the function f such that $f(x) = x^2 + \dfrac{2}{x}, \ x \neq 0$.

x	-3	-2	-1	-0.75	-0.4	0.4	0.75	1	2	3
$f(x)$	8.3	3	-1	-2.1	p	5.2	3.2	q	5	r

    a   Find the values of p, q and r, correct to 1 decimal place. *(3 marks)*

    b   Draw the graph of $y = f(x)$ for $-3 \leqslant x \leqslant 3$.

        Use a scale of 2 cm to 1 unit on the x-axis, and 1 cm to 1 unit on the y-axis. *(4 marks)*

    c   By drawing a suitable straight line, find 3 values of x where

$$f(x) = x + 3$$ *(3 marks)*

    d $x^2 + \dfrac{2}{x} = x + 3$ can be written as $x^3 + ax^2 + bx + c = 0$.

        Find the values of a, b and c. *(3 marks)*

    e   Draw a tangent to the graph of $y = f(x)$ at the point where $x = 1.5$.

        Use it to estimate the gradient of $y = f(x)$ when $x = 1.5$. *(3 marks)*

4

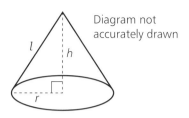

Diagram not accurately drawn

A cone has radius r, height h and slant height l.

a When $r = 4.6$ cm and $h = 11.7$ cm, show that $l = 12.57$ cm correct to 2 decimal places. *(2 marks)*

b For a cone, the curved surface area is $\pi r l$ and the volume is $\frac{1}{3}\pi r^2 h$.

For the cone in part **a**, calculate

  i the curved surface area *(2 marks)*

  ii the volume. *(2 marks)*

5

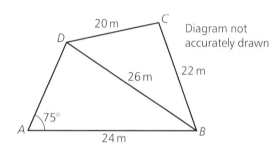

Diagram not accurately drawn

The quadrilateral, $ABCD$, represents a plot of land, with a path, BD, across it.

a **i** Using a scale of 1 : 200, draw an accurate plan of the plot of land. *(3 marks)*

  ii Measure and write down the sizes of angles ADB and BCD. *(2 marks)*

b Using trigonometry and showing all your working, calculate

  i angle ADB *(3 marks)*

  ii angle BCD *(4 marks)*

6 **a** Using a scale of 1 cm to 1 unit, draw x- and y-axes from -8 to 8. *(1 mark)*

b On the grid, plot the points $A(1, 1)$, $B(4, 3)$, $C(2, 4)$ and join them to form a triangle. *(1 mark)*

c Reflect triangle ABC in the line $y = -x$.

Label the image $A_1B_1C_1$. *(2 marks)*

d Rotate triangle $A_1B_1C_1$ through $90°$ anticlockwise about $(0, 0)$.

Label the image $A_2B_2C_2$. *(2 marks)*

e Describe fully the single transformation which maps triangle ABC onto triangle $A_2B_2C_2$. *(2 marks)*

7 $f(x) = 3x + 2$ $g(x) = \dfrac{4}{x} - 1$ $h(x) = 3^x$

    a Find the value of gf(6).   *(1 mark)*

    b Express gf(x) as a single fraction.   *(2 marks)*

    c Find $g^{-1}(x)$.   *(2 marks)*

    d Find hh(2).   *(2 marks)*

    e Find the value of x when $h(x) = g\left(\dfrac{18}{5}\right)$.   *(2 marks)*

8   The diagram shows a trapezium *ABCD* with
perpendicular height *DE*. The area of the trapezium is 133 cm².
$DC = x$ cm, $AB = (x + 4)$ cm, $DE = (2x - 1)$ cm and Angle *DAE* = 68°.

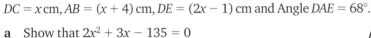

    a Show that $2x^2 + 3x - 135 = 0$
       Make all your working clear.   *(4 marks)*

    b **i** Solve the quadratic equation
         in part **a**.   *(3 marks)*

       ii Work out the length of *ED*.   *(2 marks)*

    c Calculate the length of *AD*.   *(3 marks)*

9   Four numbers have a mean of 6, a median of 6.5 and a mode of 8.

    Find the four numbers.   *(2 marks)*

10 $\mathscr{E}$ = {members of a sports club}

    A = {members who play tennis}

    B = {members who play hockey}

    $n(A \cap B) = 8$

    $n(A') = 15$

    $n(A \cup B) = 21$

    $n(\mathscr{E}) = 30$

    Find the value of:

    a $n([A \cup B]')$ *(1 mark)*

    b $n([A \cap B'])$ *(1 mark)*

11   Write the recurring decimal $0.\dot{3}2\dot{4}$ as a fraction in its lowest terms.

    Show your working clearly.   *(2 marks)*

12   A circle, centre *O*, has a radius of 6 cm.

    OA and *OB* are radii.

    Calculate the area of the shaded segment.

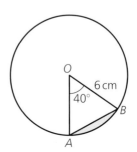

    (4 marks)

13 Show that $\dfrac{\sqrt{3} + \sqrt{2}}{\sqrt{6}} = \dfrac{\sqrt{2}}{2} + \dfrac{\sqrt{3}}{3}$ *(3 marks)*

14 The partly completed histogram below shows the time it took some adults to complete a puzzle.

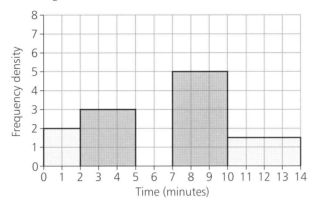

a How many adults completed the puzzle in 2 minutes or less? *(1 mark)*

b How many adults took more than 7 minutes? *(1 mark)*

c A total of 46 adults completed the puzzle.

Calculate the frequency density for the class $5 < $ time $\leqslant 7$. *(1 mark)*

15 Solve the equation $2x - 5 = 3(4x + 1)$ *(2 marks)*

16 Calculate the value of $\dfrac{3.4 \times 6.1^2}{2.7 - \sqrt{1.6}}$, giving your answer correct to 2 significant figures. *(2 marks)*

17 The height, h cm, of a ball thrown vertically upwards, t seconds after it has been thrown, is given by

$h = 5t(13 - 2t)$.

Calculate

a the maximum height of the ball *(2 marks)*

b the speed of the ball 2 seconds after it was thrown. *(2 marks)*

18 Simplify $\dfrac{4x^{-3} \times 2x^2}{6x^{-1}}$ *(2 marks)*

19 The pie chart shows the results of a survey into people's most valuable item in their house.

a 14 people answered 'cellphone.'

How many people took part in the survey? *(2 marks)*

b Four more people were surveyed.

One answered 'TV', one answered 'computer', one answered 'jewellery' and one answered 'cellphone'.

If a revised pie chart is drawn, which sector will increase in size?

Explain your answer. *(2 marks)*

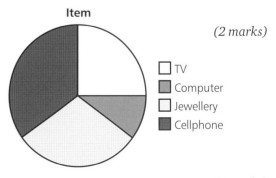

Glossary

2-way table a table used to show two different pieces of information.

acceleration the rate at which speed changes with time.

acute less than 90°.

acute-angled triangle a triangle with all of the angles less than 90°.

adjacent side the side adjacent to the known or required angle in a right-angled triangle.

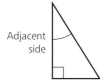

alternate angles angles formed on opposite sides of a transversal between parallel lines.

ambiguous case something that can have two different possible answers.

analogue showing a reading with a moving hand on a dial (opposite of **digital**).

angle a turn or change in direction.

angle bearings angles measured clockwise from North to describe a direction.

angle bisector a line that cuts an angle in half.

angle of depression looking down, the angle between the horizontal and the line of sight.

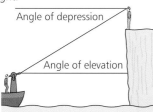

angle of elevation looking up, the angle between the line of sight and the horizontal.

annual salary amount of money a person is paid per year.

appreciate increase in value.

appreciation the increase in value of an item.

arc part of the circumference of a circle.

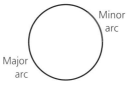

area the amount of space inside a 2-D shape.

arithmetic sequence a sequence in which the difference between consecutive terms is the same for all terms.

average speed the distance travelled in a unit of time. It is calculated by dividing the distance travelled by the time taken.

axes (singular: **axis**) fixed reference lines for the measurement of coordinates.

bar chart a chart for displaying data, using parallel bars or columns of the same width.

base number the number which is being raised to a power.

biased of an outcome that is distorted and not as expected.

BIDMAS order in which operations are performed: **B**rackets, **I**ndices (powers: squares, cubes, …), **D**ivision, **M**ultiplication, **A**ddition, **S**ubtraction.

bisect cut in half.

bonus an extra payment.

boundary edge of an area on a graph.

capacity the amount a container holds when it is full.

Cartesian coordinates two axes at right angles.

centre of enlargement the lines joining corresponding points on an object and its image all meet at the centre of enlargement.

centre of rotation fixed point at the centre of a rotation.

certain having a probability of 1.

changing the subject of a formula changing which letter is isolated on one side of the formula.

chord a straight line joining two points on the circumference of a circle.

circle the locus of a point moving at a given distance from a fixed point.

circumference the distance around the outside (perimeter) of a circle.

class boundaries the greatest and smallest values in a class.

coefficient the number in front of a quantity such as x.

collinear lying on a straight line.

common factor a factor that is common to two or more numbers or terms.

common multiple a multiple that is common to two or more numbers.

complement the complement of set A is everything outside set A.

composite function the function created when one function is followed by another.

composite shape a shape made from simple shapes.

compound interest interest which is added to the principal.

congruent having exactly the same size and shape.

consecutive next to each other.

constant of proportionality the constant value of the ratio between two proportional quantities.

continuous data data that can have any value within a range.

conversion factor a number used to convert from one unit of measurement to another.

conversion graph a graph used to convert from one unit of measurement to another.

convert change one unit of measurement to another.

corresponding angles angles formed on the same sides of a transversal between parallel lines.

cosine the length of the adjacent side of a right-angled triangle divided by the length of the hypotenuse.

cost price the original price of an item you are selling.

cross-section a face formed by cutting through an object at right angles.

cube a 3-D solid consisting of six square faces.

cube number the number you get when you multiply three lots of the number together.

cube root the inverse of cubing a number.

cubic function a function whose highest power of x is 3.

cuboid a 3-D solid consisting of six rectangular faces.

currency the unit of money that is used in a country. Different countries use different currencies.

cyclic quadrilateral a quadrilateral whose vertices lie on the circumference of a circle.

cylinder a 3-D solid with a circle of fixed radius as its cross-section.

deceleration the rate at which speed decreases with time.

decrease go down in value.

degree unit of measurement for angles.

denominator the number on the bottom of a fraction.

deposit money paid to start with.

depreciate decrease in value.

depreciation the decrease in value of an item.

diameter the distance from one point on the circumference to another point passing through the centre.

Diameter

difference the size of the step between successive terms in an arithmetic sequence.

digital showing a reading as numbers on a display (opposite of **analogue**).

direct proportion two quantities such that as one increases so does the other by the same ratio.

direct variation same as direct proportion.

directed number a positive or negative number or zero.

discontinuous having a break.

discount an amount taken off the selling price of an item.

discrete data data that can have only certain values within a range.

 E

edge the line where two faces of a solid meet.

element a member of a set.

empty set see **null set**.

enlargement a transformation in which the shape of an object stays the same, but its size usually changes.

equally likely outcomes outcomes that have the same probability.

equidistant at the same distance.

equivalent fractions fractions that are equal in value.

event a set of outcomes in probability.

expand multiply all the terms inside brackets by the term outside the brackets (opposite of **factorise**).

experimental probability the ratio of the number of times the event occurs to the total number of trials.

exponential having a constant base raised to a variable power.

expression a series of terms connected by addition and subtraction signs.

exterior angle the angle you turn through at each vertex when going round the perimeter of a polygon.

 F

face the surface of a solid which is enclosed by edges.

factor a whole number which divides exactly into another whole number.

factorise take a common factors outside a set of brackets (opposite of **expand**).

fair unbiased.

formula (plural: **formulae**) rule expressed in words or letters.

frequency the number of times a value occurs in a set of data.

function a rule which changes one number into another number.

 G

gradient a measure of how steep a line is.

grouping putting data into groups.

GST (General Sales Tax) tax added to the selling price of something.

 H

highest common factor (HCF) the largest factor which is common to two or more numbers.

hire purchase way of buying items and paying for them over a number of months.

histogram a chart that displays the frequency of data by the areas of bars.

horizontal at right angles to the vertical.

hourly rate of pay rate of pay for each hour worked.

hypotenuse the longest side of a right-angled triangle. It is always opposite the right angle.

 I

image the new shape after a transformation.

impossible having a probability of 0.

improper fraction a fraction in which the numerator is larger than the denominator.

included angle the angle between two given sides.

income tax tax paid on the money you earn.

increase go up in value.

index power of a number.

index form (**index notation**) a way of writing a number using powers.

inequality a statement about the relative size or order of two objects using $<$, $\leqslant$, $>$ and $\geqslant$.

inequation a statement similar to an equation but using $<$, $\leq$, $>$ or $\geq$ instead of $=$.

infinite continuing for ever.

instalments equal regular payments.

integers ... -5, -4, -3, -2, -1, 0, 1, 2, 3, 4, 5, ...

intercept where a line crosses an axis.

interest the charge for borrowing or lending money.

interior angle the angle inside a polygon.

interquartile range the difference between the upper and lower quartiles.

intersection
1. a point where two graphs meet.
2. a set that is made up of all the elements that belong to both of two different sets.

inverse something that is reversed in order or effect.

inverse proportion a relation between two variables, in which one variable increases as the other decreases.

irrational number a number that cannot be written as a fraction.

like terms terms containing the same variables raised to the same power, which can be combined by adding or subtracting.

line of symmetry the fold line when a 2-D shape can be folded so that one half fits exactly over the other.

line segment the part of a line joining two points.

line symmetry symmetry in which a 2-D shape divides a shape into two congruent halves which are mirror images of each other.

linear equation an equation that does not contain any powers or roots of x or y such as x^2 or $\sqrt{y}$.

line a one-dimensional figure extending infinitely in both directions.

loss the difference between what you sell something for and what you buy it for.

lower bound the smallest possible value of a rounded quantity.

lower quartile the value one quarter of the way from the lowest value.

lowest common denominator the lowest common multiple of the denominators of two or more fractions.

lowest common multiple (LCM) the lowest multiple that is common to two or more numbers.

magnitude the size of a vector.

mapping the process which changes one number into another number.

mean a way of calculating how much each value would be if all the values were shared equally.

measure of dispersion a measure of how spread out data are.

median the middle value, when data are put in order.

membership all the elements in a set.

mirror line a **line of symmetry**.

mixed number a fractions that consists of a whole number part and a fractional part.

modal of the score or class with the highest frequency.

modal class the class with the highest frequency.

mode the score with the highest frequency.

multiple the product of a number and an integer.

multiplier method multiplying a quantity by a fraction representing a ratio.

mutually exclusive having no outcomes in common.

N

natural numbers the counting numbers, 1, 2, 3, 4, 5, ...

negative integer any negative whole number.

net a 2-D pattern that can be cut out and folded to form a 3-D shape.

non-terminating decimal a decimal that does not end.

nth term counting from the 1st term in a sequence, the term in position n.

null set a set that contains no elements.

numerator the number on top of a fraction.

O

object the original shape before a transformation.

obtuse greater than $90°$ but less than $180°$

obtuse-angled triangle a triangle with one of the angles more than $90°$.

odometer an instrument that measures the distance a car has travelled.

operations $+$, $-$, $\times$, $\div$.

opposite side the side opposite to the known or required angle in a right-angled triangle.

Opposite side

order of rotational symmetry the number of different positions in which a shape looks the same during a complete turn.

ordered pair a pair that go together in order, like coordinates.

origin the point (0, 0) where graph axes cross, where both coordinates are zero.

outcome result.

overtime extra hours worked.

P

parallel parallel lines are the same distance apart everywhere along their length.

per annum every year.

perimeter the total distance around the sides of a shape.

perpendicular at right angles ($90°$).

perpendicular bisector a line that cut a line in half at right angles.

pictogram a way of representing data using pictures and a key.

pie chart a circular chart showing frequencies as sectors of a circle.

point the intersection of two lines.

polygon a two-dimensional shape with straight sides.

position vector a vector from the orig (0, 0) to a point.

position-to-term rule a rule for a sequence linking the term number to the value of that term.

positive integer any positive whole number.

possibility diagram a diagram in which dots represent possible events.

power the number of times a base number is multiplied.

prime number a number that has exactly two factors: itself and one.

principal the amount of money invested.

prism a 3-D solid whose cross-section is the same throughout its length.

probability scale a scale on which probabilities are shown.

profit the difference between what you sell something for and what you buy it for.

proportion comparing one part to the total amount.

quadratic function a function in which x^2 is the highest power of x.

qualitative descriptive but not numerical.

quantitative numerical.

radius (plural: **radii**) the distance from one point on the circumference to the centre.

Radius

range the difference between the largest item and the smallest item in a set of data.

rate the rate of interest per year for borrowing or lending money.

rate of change the change in one variable compared with the change in another variable.

ratio comparing two or more quantities with each other.

rational number any number that can be written in the form $\frac{p}{q}$, where p and q are integers.

raw data data as collected before being grouped.

real number any rational or irrational number.

reciprocal a fraction turned upside down.

reciprocal function a graph involving a reciprocal such as $y = \frac{1}{x}$.

recurring decimal a decimal with an infinite number of decimal places, in which a digit, or group of digits, eventually repeats.

reflection a transformation that gives an image which looks like the reflection of the object in a mirror.

reflex greater than 180° but less than 360°.

region an area on a graph, grid or map.

regular having all sides equal and all angles equal.

relative frequency
$$\frac{\text{the number of outcomes for the event}}{\text{total number of trials}}.$$

reverse percentage working back from a percentage to find the original quantity.

right angle an angle of 90°.

right-angled triangle a triangle with one of the angles 90°.

rotation turning an object through a given angle about a fixed point.

rotational symmetry looking exactly the same after a rotation of less than 360°.

rounding rewriting a number to a given degree of accuracy.

rule a general statement.

 S

sample space diagram a table showing all the possible outcomes.

scalar a quantity with size but no direction.

scale drawing accurate drawing that shows the exact shape but does not use the actual size.

scale factor a number that tells you how many times bigger the object is than the image.

sector a region of a circle cut off by two radii and an arc.

segment a region of a circle cut off by a chord and an arc.

self-inverse being its own inverse.

selling price the price you sell something for.

semicircle half a circle.

sequence a set of numbers or patterns with a given rule or pattern.

set a collection of objects or numbers, usually having something in common.

significant figures the digits of a number, starting from the first non-zero digit.

similar having the same shape, with lengths in the same proportion

simple interest the charge for borrowing or lending money. $I = \frac{PRT}{100}$.

simplest form
1. the form with the smallest possible whole numbers in the numerator and the denominator of a fraction, or the smallest possible whole numbers in a ratio.
2. in algebra, reducing an expression into the fewest terms.

simplifying collecting the like terms.

simultaneous equations two equations with two unknowns.

sine the length of the opposite side of a right-angled triangle divided by the length of the hypotenuse.

sine rule a rule connecting sides and angles of a non-right-angled triangle. $\frac{a}{\sin A} = \frac{b}{\sin B} = \frac{c}{\sin C}$.

solid a three-dimensional shape.

solve find the solution(s) to an equation.

square number the result of multiplying an integer by itself.

square root that which must be squared to equal a number.

standard form a way of writing very large and very small numbers using a number between 1 and 10 multiplied by a power of 10.

subset if every element of A is also in B, then A is a subset of B written $A \subset B$.

substitution replacing the letters in an expression with numbers to find its value.

surface area the total area of the faces of a solid.

tally chart a method of keeping count of data.

tangent
1. a straight line that touches a curve at only one point.
2. the length of the opposite side divided by the length of the adjacent side in a right-angled triangle.

term one item in a numerical or algebraic expression.

terminating decimal a decimal with a finite number of decimal places.

term-to-term rule a rule for a sequence linking one term to the value of the next term.

transformation a change of the position or the size of a shape.

transforming changing the subject of a formula.

translation a transformation in which all points of an object move the same distance in the same direction.

transversal a line that cuts two or more parallel lines.

tree diagram a tree-shaped diagram that shows all the outcomes for each event, and the probabilities.

trial an experiment that is repeated a large number of times.

trigonometry a method of finding lengths of sides and sizes of angles in triangles.

union a set that is made up of all the elements of two or more sets.

unit vector a vector that is one unit long.

unitary method finding the value of one unit of a quantity.

unitary ratio any ratio in the form $1 : n$.

Universal Set the set containing all elements to be considered.

unknown a value you are trying to find.

unlike terms terms containing different variables or combinations of variables.

upper bound the greatest possible value of a rounded quantity.

upper quartile the value three-quarters of the way from the lowest value.

variable a quantity that can take different values.

VAT (Value Added Tax) tax added to the selling price of something.

vector a quantity possessing magnitude and direction.

Venn diagram a way of showing how elements of a set are grouped.

vertex (plural: **vertices**) a point where three or more edges of a solid meet.

vertical at right angles to the horizontal.

volume the amount of space inside a 3-D shape.

weekly wage the amount of money a person is paid per week.

x-axis a line running from left to right used to identify positions on a grid.

x-coordinate the first number in a pair of coordinates identifying the position of a point relative to the x-axis.

y-axis a line running from top to bottom used to identify positions on a grid.

y-coordinate the second number in a pair of coordinates identifying the position of a point relative to the y-axis.